Making Room to Pray

Making Room to Pray

Terry Teykl

Prayer Point Press

Prayer Point Press
2100 N. Carrolton Dr.
Muncie, IN 47304

Phone: 765 759-0215
Fax: 765 759-5857
To order, call toll-free: 1-888 656-6067
www.prayerpointpress.com

DEDICATION

Dedicated to Ted and Delores Wyatt who
have prayed for me and helped Renewal
Ministries promote corporate prayer in the
body of Christ.

Contents

Introduction

Years ago my wife and I traveled to Korea. While we were there, we witnessed the people of God praying in intense, fervent prayer. In spite of the fact that their churches are among the largest in the world, and winning new converts daily, they pray. They pray as though their lives and the life of their church depend on it. They are radically dependent on God.

We visited Prayer Mountain where people go on their days off or vacations to pray in the prayer closets. We attended morning prayer meetings and saw in front of the altar a floor area as large as a football field filled with intercessors on their faces before God. The huge sanctuary was packed and the people prayed with such intensity that it sounded like an enormous bee hive. The more souls they win to Christ the louder and longer they pray. They believe in the dynamics of prayer and their country is being won to Christ because of it!

When Kay and I returned to Houston and were driving home from the airport, I began to notice that church after church was locked up tight. My heart was grieved because our beautiful facilities, built for the glory of God, stood ready to be the houses of prayer that Jesus spoke of. But, for the most part, they were closed six days a week.

God spoke to my heart that day and I decided to make room to pray at the church I was serving. We opened a 24-hour prayer room and it altered our church and greatly affected our city. While serving at Aldersgate United Methodist Church, we were blessed to see a large number of new souls won to Jesus. I know souls were won as the result of the hours of faithful intercession that were offered in the prayer room.

Since that day in 1991 the heart of our ministry has been to help local churches launch prayer rooms. All across the country hundreds of churches are now involved in prayer room intercession. Soon we hope to see a network of prayer rooms tied into the nerve center at the World Prayer Center in Colorado Springs, Colorado.

The vision to have a method of communicating between prayer rooms has been a part of the vision that God gave me from the start. Now it appears that the vision is going to be made possible by the World Prayer Center.

The network will allow us to communicate global prayer concerns directly to the local church. It will also serve as a messenger of encouragement and inspiration to the prayer room intercessors as they wage war on their knees.

In addition, the local prayer room will be able to report answers to prayer and community breakthroughs. As I travel I receive so many wonderful stories of how God moves in response to prayer. The network will allow these testimonies to be reported beyond their local communities.

God is doing a new thing in corporate prayer! As you study this manual, pray that God will impart the vision for a prayer room in your church. Pray that many souls will be won, many hurting people will find the comfort and peace of God, marriages will be saved, and missionaries protected through the faithful intercession of the saints.

Chapter One

The Upper Room Principle

In Acts 1:14 we read "They all joined together constantly in prayer, along with the women and Mary the mother of Jesus, and his brothers."

How amazing!

Jesus had just been resurrected from the dead! He had just conquered sin, Satan and the grave. On the road to Emmaus he had appeared to two of his disciples. Later they said, "Were not our hearts burning within us while he talked with us on the road and opened the scriptures to us?" (Luke 24:32). Then Jesus appeared to the disciples in the upper room and said to them, "Peace be with you ... As the Father has sent me, I am sending you" (John 20:19, 21). He gave them the message of salvation for the world—yet, we find them here constantly praying in the upper room.

> Surely they wanted to surge into the world preaching, rather than waiting upon the Lord!

How amazing!

They were not preaching or teaching. They were not organizing; they were not training leaders. They were praying! They were not going over the budget because they did not have one. They were not writing scriptures or studying them. They were praying! They were not planning or setting goals; they were not talking over past events. They were praying!

> His mandate to them was to hold a prayer meeting and do nothing but pray.

What amazing restraint. Surely they wanted to surge into the world preaching, rather than waiting upon the Lord!

Why did they wait?

In Luke 24:49, Jesus' last command was to "stay in the city until you have been clothed with power from on high." His mandate to them was to hold a prayer meeting and do nothing but pray. So here they were, constantly praying in what was known as the upper room. This room is mentioned in Mark 14:15 and Luke 22:12. The upper room may have been the place for the Last Supper and the resurrection appearances. Some believe it was the home of Mary, the mother of John Mark (Acts 12:12). It was a large room because at one time there were 120 people gathered there (Acts 1:15).

This upper room was their prayer center. It was their designated place of corporate prayer. People were evidently coming and going to pray. Some would leave and others would come, but we get the impression that people were there praying around the clock. New believers, women, Jesus' family and the apostles were there constantly praying.

We read in the King James version they were of "one accord." Also in Acts 2:1, 2:46, and 5:12 we see that they were of "one accord." This means they were in an agreement of prayer. They were focused in their praying, even though they were a diverse lot and represented different levels of spiritual maturity. They all wanted the same thing in prayer.

Their personal agendas had taken a back seat to what Jesus wanted. They were not arguing for rank or position—they were of one heart, one mind, one purpose—they were in one accord on their knees! Therefore, this upper room was a place of focused prayer in preparation for their mission. The early church came together to pray God's agenda and not just their own.

A Room Full of Miracles

Perhaps some came to see Jesus. Acts 1:3 says,

> *After his suffering, he showed himself to these men and gave many convincing proofs that he was alive. He appeared to them over a period of forty days and spoke about the kingdom of God.*

Wow! Who wanted to plan or preach or do anything other than pray? Jesus could have appeared at any moment; therefore, they wanted to wait and be prepared to worship. This room, no doubt, was full of expectations. These people were on tip-toe to see the risen Lord and the things he might do.

Notes

Then in Acts 2 it happened. "When the day of Pentecost came they were all together in one place. Suddenly a sound like the blowing of a violent wind came from heaven and filled the whole house where they were sitting." It happened—in this closet room of prayer their "clothing" arrived. They were now dressed for the task. The Holy Spirit was poured out on them. They went in to pray and came out to preach. They went in to wait, and they came out to serve. They went in to find and left to give the life of Jesus to a dying world!

> This little band of people with no buildings, no money, no tapes or books emerged from this room and turned the world right-side up.

This upper room-prayer room became a launching pad for the church's mission. Profound and exciting things happened after the Spirit came upon them. This little band of people with no buildings, no money, no tapes and no books emerged from this room to turn the world right-side up.

The early church began as a prayer meeting. Jesus' last command, "stay ... until you have been clothed with power" (Luke 24:40) became their first concern. However, in the process of waiting, the early church discovered something that I call the Upper Room Principle: When God gives us a great task he expects us to seek him with all our heart and soul and strength before we endeavor to do that task because we must realize completely that his Spirit, not might or power, will accomplish this task (Zechariah:4-6). This principle became deeply ingrained in the disciples.

Michael Green says it well:

> *...it is through prayer that God is free to reach and use us. If we do things for God without praying, he cannot afford the risk of allowing us to succeed. For we would get proud and would be hardened in our conviction that activism, not dependence on God, is the way for Christians to serve the Lord.*[1]

This Upper Room Principle means that first and foremost we should focus on the Lord—not just the work he has given us. Another has said it this way; "We are committed to the Lord of the work, not the work of the Lord."

Therefore, the early believers were to seek him "constantly," and they did. This principle would be their prayerful norm for the rest of Acts. For example, in Acts 4 when the authorities warned them to no longer preach in Jesus' name, the apostles met and "raised their voices together in prayer to God," for courage and direction, and as they sought him, he "shook" them loose from their fear by his Spirit. Again in Acts 12:5 when Herod had captured Peter meaning to do him harm; we read "the church was earnestly praying to God for him." The answer—a freed Peter—came knocking on the upper room door! Someone has said that the angel fetched Peter, but prayer fetched the angel.

> Jesus was radically dependent on the Father for everything. Can we be any less?

The Upper Room Principle calls us to seek the Lord as we start his work, as we do his work and as we complete his work. This principle guided our Lord himself. He rose early to seek the Father (Mark 1:35-

Notes

37). He often withdrew to lonely places (Luke 5:16), and he even spent the whole night seeking God (Luke 6:12). Jesus was radically dependent on the Father for everything. Can we be any less?

Jesus gave the early church an impossible task: preach the Good News, proclaim his forgiveness, heal the sick, cast out demons, raise the dead and establish his kingdom upon the earth. He commissioned them to "Go! Make disciples! Baptize them and teach them my words" and he gave them only two resources: a new life in his name and a mandate to wait upon him in prayer (Luke 24:40). So they waited in prayer—focusing on him alone. And then it happened. Acts 2 describes the Pentecost when they received their marching orders, and out they went. It happened just like he told them it would. Lives were changed, conversions came, the church was born. Out they would go and back they would come to their source and wait again for holy unction and direction. Following the Upper Room Principle bridged the gap so his power could reach them and the gospel could penetrate the pagan world.

> They had been "shut up with God" but when they came forth nothing could "shut them up..."

They would inhale this power and exhale this breath of life as they preached in the marketplaces and homes of Lystra and Derbe. The oxygen of the kingdom came through the Upper Room Principle. I call this prayer-evangelism. The early believers had an evangelistic message, evangelistic methods and harvest results. Yet, all of this was soaked in and saturated with prayer—all kinds of prayer, at all times, with everybody praying. Prayer was their priority.

Later in Acts 6 we see this principle threatened. The church was growing, and the disciples were neglecting prayer. So they elected deacons to be responsible for the daily distribution of food and said, we "will give our attention to prayer and the ministry of the word" (Acts 6:4). Then we read the results: "So the word of God spread. The number of disciples in Jerusalem increased rapidly" (Acts 6:7).

Let me sum it up. Church historians seldom debate this fact: the first disciples who went into that upper room were locked in, fearful and intimidated, but something happened in that room! They came out with such boldness and conviction that thousands of people came to the Lord. They had been "shut up with God" but when they came forth nothing could "shut them up for God and the sake of the Gospel." And so they found Jesus' words true:

Ask and it will be given to you. For everyone who asks receives; he who seeks finds; and to him who knocks, the door will be opened ... how much more will your Father in heaven give the Holy Spirit to those who ask him! (Luke 11:9-10, 13b).

The Place Where Prayer Can Happen

A significant part of this Upper Room Principle is having a place where prayer can happen—a room, a site, a meeting hall—just as the disciples met in the upper room. In this actual room people can pray, cry, petition, wait, be quiet, intercede and believe to receive from God. The early believers were disciplined to know the importance of having a place to practice the principle of seeking God. And as the church

Notes

grew there were other fixed "places of prayer"(Acts 16:13, 16). The place of prayer became essential to the practice of corporate prayer. It is my conviction that many churches today are rediscovering this Upper Room Principle as it pertains to evangelism and church growth. And as a part of this new movement of prayer, "places" for personal and corporate prayer are being established all over the land.

> In such a place...pleas for cleansing can be offered up, visions can be imparted, dreams can be given.

Making Room to Pray is written with the intent of helping you establish such a place of prayer in your home or church or ministry area. Call it a prayer center, prayer room, prayer chapel, or prayer closet—it does not matter. What is important is that there is a place where it can happen—where people can come regularly to have specific information to pray from—to pray alone or together, to record the results, to be trained and equipped for city-wide intercession and to wait upon the Lord as they did in Acts 1:14. In such a place corporate repentance can happen, pleas for cleansing can be offered up, visions can be imparted, dreams can be given, the "price can be prayed."

I believe that city-wide prayer will require such a place or places as we take our cities for God. Prayer centers can serve other purposes as places of quiet, personal devotion or meditation, etc. Yet, my purpose is to accept the Great Commission. The questions I pose are: How can we take the city? What strongholds must be pulled down? Can we come against prejudice, immorality, murder, rebellion? How can we pray for unity in the body? In Jesus' Name what are we to bind and loosen? Who are the missionaries? Where are they? Can we map our praying? Is there a good list of church and city leaders to pray over specifically?

Making Room to Pray will share some ideas from churches and ministries who are doing this kind of intercession. The intent is to encourage creativity and challenge you to build your own prayer room. I will also share why I believe it is a worthwhile effort to invite the Holy Spirit to bring new life and power to existing ministries, as well as to bring souls to Christ. Some prayer centers have a phone ministry; I will also offer some insights about training people to participate in an intercessory telephone ministry.

Imagine right now a group of people praying at your church over the local high school. Imagine what a difference could be made in your church or neighborhood through the prayers of people committing to pray one hour a week. Imagine having someone properly trained at your church to take the call of a distressed person or runaway child. Imagine a corporate prayer group praying two or three times a day in your prayer center interceding by name for those who need healing. Imagine prayer warriors at your church continually waiting upon God in praise for all he has done as recorded in that room. This type of praying is happening all over the land. It could happen in your church. Make room to pray and see what happens.

Notes

Brainstorm

Create a list of physical spaces where your church might create a prayer room. For now, try to generate as many ideas as possible and don't worry about the practicality of your suggestions.

1.

2.

3.

4.

5.

6.

Chapter 2

Who's Making Room to Pray?

Churches and ministries are finding places today to pray for the evangelization of their communities. And the variety and scope of these prayer centers are as diverse as the ministries themselves.

For example, Reinhard Bonnke is an African evangelist who conducts large evangelistic crusades all over the continent of Africa. At a crusade in Bulawayo, Zimbabwe, they set up an outdoor platform with speakers and lights, and the people came to stand in front of the platform. Behind the platform, about a

> Fifty thousand people came forward and more than 10,000 of them made decisions for Christ.

100 yards away, a tent was set up for prayer. Four times a day the intercessors gathered there to pray before and during the crusade. People came from all walks of life—men, women, old and young. They came with one intent—to pray that God would grant souls to be saved.

What was the end result of that crusade? Fifty thousand people came forward and more than 10,000 of them made decisions for Christ. This type of corporate prayer goes on in all of Reinhard Bonnke's crusades. They write,

This facet of the ministry largely goes unnoticed in the multi-thousand crowds, the drama of the huge altar calls, and the signs and wonders which follow. The victories demonstrated in the stadiums and large crusades, however, are planned and executed in the realm of prayer. Here, unseen by the masses, the real battles are fought and won. From the prayer halls, the power of God is released to bring about the success of the crusades—all to the glory of God.

They attribute the success of their crusades to the great prayer force going on during the crusade. Their prayer room is a tent set up in the middle of nowhere, yet it serves well the purpose of enlisting people to pray. Again, the Upper Room Principle is that as we seek him, God is able to bless our efforts in such a way that God and only God can be glorified.

> The Upper Room Principle is that as we seek him, God is able to bless our efforts in such a way that God and only God can be glorified.

Now, such a tent just does not "happen." Plans are made ahead of time, intercessors are recruited, time and much effort are spent getting them in place. The results of the crusade are reported back to the intercessors to encourage them and bless their praying. They are told how to pray and given specific instructions. The end result is thousands upon thousands of people coming to Christ.

A different approach to prayer center intercession is Paul Cho's Prayer Mountain near Seoul, Korea. Years ago a cemetery was given to the Full Gospel Central Church in Seoul. They turned this land into a prayer center. Now thousands of people go to Prayer Mountain to pray privately and corporately. The chapel seats 10,000 people while "Prayer grottos" in the sides of the mountain serve as places where people can go and seek God individually. Pastor Cho says on average 3,000 people fast and pray there daily. In 1984 more than 300,000 people registered to come to Prayer Mountain. Hotel accommodations are available for people who want to spend several days. My wife and I were there in 1984 and saw hundreds of people on their prayer mats seeking God and waiting upon him. For me, seeing so many seek God so diligently was an unforgettable experience.

Other such prayer centers can be found in Korea. The largest Methodist Church in the world, Kwang Lim, is in Korea is pastored by Dr. Sundo Kim. This church has a 7.5 million dollar prayer center located one hour from Seoul. The prayer center complex consists of an auditorium, prayer benches and personal prayer rooms. The auditorium is made of brick, stone and glass and can seat 5,000 people with facilities to feed and sleep 800 people. Scattered about the grounds are kneeling benches for private prayer. Also, 104 tiny prayer rooms are available for private prayer. They have "occupancy" lights that indicate when a room is occupied and special security doors that can only be opened from the inside. Pastor Kim spends all day at the center on Saturday preparing for the four services on Sunday.

Closer to home, the Oral Roberts Prayer Tower is one example of a telephone prayer ministry. They receive an average of 1,500 calls a week. A group of trained intercessors is available around the clock to pray over callers' requests. Other national ministries also have telephone ministries—Robert Schuller, Pat Robertson, and the United

Methodist Church for example. The United Methodist Church has an Upper Room in Nashville Tennessee that receives over 13,000 calls per month. From prayer tents to prayer towers, the Upper Room Principle is being utilized with variety and diversity across the world.

The Newest Prayer Movement

Yet the newest prayer room movement is among local churches. There are as many styles of prayer centers as there are flavors of churches. Galloway United Methodist Church in Franklin, Pennsylvania built a prayer room with its own combination lock entrance separate from the church. Pastor Dave Hampson reports that thirty people pray regularly at the prayer room and they are now planning a door-hanger campaign to collect prayer requests from the community. The prayer room at Galloway is both comfortable and well organized.

> The newest prayer room movement is among local churches.

The prayer room of Englewood Baptist Church in Rocky Mount, North Carolina is the nerve center of all that goes on at the church. The prayer room is open 24 hours a day, seven days a week and houses over 2,000 prayer requests at any given time. Intercessors can sign up to pray one hour a week, as a substitute or as part of the "at-home" intercessors. The success of their prayer room is measured and reported through monthly updates, praises and new requests.

Kay Bindrim, Englewood's prayer coordinator, reports that,

> *" The Spirit of God is always fresh and we see his hand at work each time we step through the doors of the prayer room. Every week we see praise reports of new souls won into the Kingdom of God. We see runaways found, dire circumstances and impossible situations turned into victories."*

Pastors George and Sandy McClosky and the Glen's Valley United

Methodist Church hired an artist to do a beautiful symbolic mural in their prayer room. The mural depicts their church, community, country and the world. Current prayer information is available at each station of the mural to help people pray specifically.

Many churches are investing time and resources in developing more elaborate prayer rooms. One example of this type of prayer center in a local church is the Hillcrest Church in Dallas, Texas where Dr. Morris Sheats pastors. Their prayer room is an entirely separate building. Two rooms in the front of the building are the intercessory prayer rooms. Each of these rooms has two television sets. At 4:30 p.m. each day the televisions are fed prayer requests and answers. One set monitors the requests of Hillcrest Church only, and the other shows the prayer concerns of the Metroplex area. In the other prayer room a television lists the concerns of the state and world, and the last television publishes the praise reports. As people come to pray in a comfortable surrounding, they pray in an up-to-date manner over current prayer requests. Behind these two rooms is a chapel with room for corporate prayer at noon, Monday through Friday. Off to the side of the chapel is a small apartment for men who take 24-hour shifts to be there to wait upon God. These 90 men are called Levites. Upstairs are small prayer cubicles for people to use for times of solitude and personal prayer.

This church has made room to pray in a unique and creative manner. Their prayer center is more complex than most and cost several thousand dollars to build. However, Hillcrest Church is growing and Dr. Sheats says it is because of prayer.

Another dynamic prayer room ministry is at the Champion Forest Baptist Church in Houston, Texas. Their prayer room is open twelve hours a day, seven days a week. Some 175 intercessors volunteer to pray one hour or more each week in the prayer room. This prayer center has eight prayer stations making it possible for several people to pray in the center at the same time. Each station has a unique focus plus information and prayer cards detailing the needs related to the focus. Those entering first kneel at an altar rail to prepare themselves. They then move to the crisis station where the greatest and most immediate needs are posted for each hour. Other stations include the pastoral staff, missionaries, pregnant women and those with newborn children, social issues, unsaved friends and neighbors and church members.

> "When we work, we work, but when we pray, God works."

They also receive about 150 calls a week on the church's prayer line. The calls are answered by trained intercessors, and the person calling receives prayer right there on the telephone. Then their need is placed on a prayer need card, and it goes to the appropriate prayer station. Prayer-grams are often sent to those who are prayed for as a note of encouragement.

Champion Forest Baptist Church has grown from 500 members in 1978 to 9,500 in 1998. Pastor Damon Shook explains their growth by saying, "Prayer undergirds everything." He adds, "When we work, we work, but when we pray, God works." It is also interesting to note that now more than 1,000 Southern Baptist churches like Champion Forest have an intercessory prayer room, and all of them are dynamic, growing churches.

The Kansas City Fellowship in Kansas City, Missouri, has a well-developed ministry of prayer in each of its several locations. Each prayer center contains information, pictures, current newspaper clippings and the names of people needing prayer. People meet in the prayer center at 6 a.m., 12 noon, and 6 p.m. to pray for an hour or two. Generally a staff member, leading from a microphone in the front, will pray from a passage of scripture addressing the needs of the church, city, and nation. These corporate prayer times begin with praise and worship. Also, three or four different people may lead the prayer time. Some sit, some lie down, some stand, others move along the wall praying for the needs listed. From time to time they may sit someone down in a chair and pray for them personally. Their pastor, Mike Bickle, says that their growth is due to prayer. With only a few in 1980, they have now grown to more than 8,000.

Pastor Bickle believes God is restoring the church today to walk in holiness, power and supernatural works. He also sees community-wide prayer as essential to community-wide revival. They help sponsor "Concerts of Prayer" in which churches of various denominations come together to intercede for the city. They have plans to build a city-wide prayer center where a few to as many as hundreds will be able to pray. Their plans are bold, and their commitment to pray is rooted in the conviction that through prayer, the city will be won.

Another unique prayer ministry is developing in the home. Some

Notes

Christian families are building personal, home prayer rooms. They pray together at the church prayer room and because of the quiet atmosphere and the informed focus, they now want such a place in their home.

One little girl asked, "Daddy, why can't we have a room like this at our house?" So, mom and dad cleared out their master bedroom closet and created a prayer room for their family. These rooms are usually patterned after the corporate prayer rooms. Other Christians are building altar areas in their homes for family devotions and intercessory prayer.

What Would Simeon or Anna Find at Your Church?

Could it be that a new movement is sweeping churches and Christian homes? Whereas churches have been locked up and the television has captured center stage in the home, people are now wanting to find a place to pray personally and corporately for their church and city. Could it be that more and more people are realizing that it is going to take serious prayer to turn the tide of evil in our communities?

> To succeed in and accomplish that which God calls us to do, we must pray.

Some are wanting more. They desire a real move of God with a revival of holiness and people coming to the Lord. Such a desire will cause people to seek out places and prayer forces to bring about a latter day revival. I believe we are going to see the advent of many unique, creative places of prayer in this generation because we are finally realizing that it is not by might nor by power, but by his spirit that this generation will be won to Christ. Make room to pray and see if God will send a Simeon or an Anna as in Luke 2. The Bible says Simeon "was righteous and devout. He was waiting for the consolation of Israel, and the Holy Spirit was upon him." (Luke 2:25). And of Anna we read that, "She never left the temple but worshiped night and day, fasting and praying" (Luke 2:37). If Simeon or Anna were to come to your church, would there be a place for them to stay and pray at some length?

The churches and ministries I have described are discovering the Upper Room Principle the early church knew. To succeed in and accomplish that which God calls us to do, we must pray. We must seek him with all our heart, soul and mind. Prayer is a vital means of realizing the kingdom of God. This is especially true of evangelism. Church growth needs to be more than setting goals, adopting methods and developing a good advertising campaign to attract people to the building. I lament as I read books on church growth principles that often prayer is left out. Church growth principles such as good worship, visitation, community analyses, building programs, staff considerations, location, parking and children's ministries are valuable. However, prayer before, during and after the whole of the Great Commission is crucial to God getting the glory. Prayer saves the church from becoming just a well-oiled machine printing bulletins, conducting services and organizing ice-cream socials. Programs without prayer cause us to be human-centered, human-powered and human-dependent.

The early church knew well that if they were to succeed it would be through prayer and the leading of the Holy Spirit. Jesus set this standard of prayer both in example and word. He prayed in the beginning (Mark 1:35), and the crowds came. He prayed often during his ministry (Luke 5:16). He prayed in the choosing of strategy and

Notes

disciples (Luke 4:42, 6:12). He prayed in the end (Luke 22:39). From the cross he prayed (Luke 23:34). He told them, "My house will be called a house of prayer" (Matthew 21:13).

> Prayer is not man getting his will done in heaven, it is God getting His will done on earth.

Jesus set the example and instructed his followers to do likewise. He told them to go to Jerusalem and wait until they were "clothed with power" (Luke 24:49), and they obeyed: "They all joined together constantly in prayer, along with the women and Mary the mother of Jesus, and his brothers" (Acts 1:14). Prayer is mentioned 33 times in the book of Acts. As you read between the lines in Acts you see a church that had little to distract it—their life in the Lord was one of simple and constant devotion. Prayer-evangelism was their first priority! Their meetings did not open or close with prayer. They were nothing but prayer! And so the gospel spread.

Prayer Is Not An Aladdin's Lamp

Churches with prayer centers and organized prayer ministries are also discovering it is biblical to pray for the lost. Too often prayer has become human-centered in the church. We see prayer as a means of getting what we need. The Bible becomes an Aladdin's lamp to rub in faith to ask the Holy Spirit genie to grant a better golf game, or good weather or a new house. Warren Wiersbe is right: "Prayer is not man getting his will done in heaven, it is God getting his will done on earth."[2] When we pray, we need the Lord's agenda. To pray for the lost and for the salvation of our cities is his agenda.

The Bible is full of examples of this kind of prayer-evangelism. In Numbers 11:1-2 Moses prayed for God not to consume the unbelieving, complaining Israelites. In Numbers 14:9 he cried out to God saying, "In accordance with your great love, forgive the sin of these people ..." Samuel prayed in 1 Samuel 12:23-25 for God to spare an idolatrous Israel. Jeremiah prayed for those condemned (Jeremiah 7:13-16, 14:10-13). Hezekiah prayed, "May the Lord, who is good, pardon everyone who sets his heart on seeking God"(2 Chronicles 30:17-20).

Daniel interceded for the lost in Daniel 9:17-19. Jesus himself prayed and wept over Jerusalem (Luke 19:41-44). When Stephen was being stoned, he prayed for his accusers: "Lord, do not hold this sin against them" (Acts 7:60). Paul had a prayer burden for his own people (Romans 9:2). And Paul admonishes us in 1 Timothy 2:1-4, "I urge you, then, first of all, that requests, prayers, intercession and thanksgiving be made for everyone. This is good, and pleases God our Savior, who wants all men to be saved and to come to a knowledge of the truth." It is very biblical to stand in the gap for the unsaved. I will share more examples later, but suffice it to say that one of the Father's most important agendas is for us to spend time seeking him for the lost and for ways to reach them.

Prayer-Evangelism Doesn't Just Happen—It Takes Work

Congregations like Full Gospel Central and Champion Forest Baptist are discovering that prayer is something that can be mobilized in a local church for evangelistic results. Like Sunday school or the annual pledge campaign, corporate prayer can have intent, organization and direction. Prayer centers don't just happen. They re-

quire as much work as any other ministry in the church. Prayer too often has been taken for granted and left up to just anybody who might do it. This is not so in praying churches.

> A church cannot afford a boring prayer ministry any more than it can afford a boring worship service.

Prayer-evangelism requires work. It requires someone to lead the movement—a praying leader who motivates others, (this person need not be the pastor). It requires purpose and direction—prayer plans give limit, scope and direction to intercession in a local church. Questions need to be answered, such as, "When do we begin?" "Where will we pray?" "How many prayer ministries will we have?" Praying churches will have prayer budgets because material is needed for training and maintenance of the ministry. Recruitment is crucial to enlisting people to pray—sign-up methods are orchestrated and accountability is built into the ministry. The work of prayer-evangelism can be compared to the work required for a good youth program.

Each church may provide its own unique format as a praying church. Creativity and variety add interest and enjoyment to a local corporate prayer ministry. A church cannot afford a boring prayer ministry any more than it can afford a boring worship service. All forms and kinds of prayer are needed to claim a city for God. Prayer rooms or centers are one of the ways that make prayer visible in the local church and community.

God is doing a new work in the area of corporate prayer today. Churches all over the land are building and establishing prayer centers. They are popping up in tents, special buildings and rejuvenated chapels. Many of these ministries are reaching people for Christ. People are praying for their lost communities and they are being changed; prayer is pushing back the powers of darkness; the Holy Spirit is coming on the unsaved with greater conviction. And all of this is happening because prayer is happening. No longer is prayer taken for granted, no longer is it left out. New effort, quality time and first class consideration are being devoted to the vital mandate to pray.

Brainstorm

List the current prayer
ministries of your church.

1.

2.

3.

What percentage of your congregation is involved
in a prayer ministry?

Envision what a prayer room in your church might
look like. What physical attributes such as furniture, lighting or decor might enhance a persons
time in the prayer room?

Chapter Three

Corporate Prayer and the Holy Spirit

The Holy Spirit is the church's Evangelist. He is the sent promise of the Father upon the church to enable and empower us to win a lost world to Christ. Without this Evangelist there can be no church growth. He sets the agenda for evangelism. And when we pray we invite this Evangelist to come and do his supernatural work in the church and the city. Prayer evangelism bridges the gap between a lost world and the church's mission. In this chapter I want to highlight the work of the Holy Spirit in evangelism and also show how prayer brings the Holy Spirit upon our task.

I believe there are eight effects of the Holy Spirit on the church when prayer targets the Great Commission. Also, I believe there are 10 major works of the Holy Spirit on the unsaved. And when we pray, these effects and works are evident. Paul writes, "...because our gospel came to you not simply with words, but also with power, with the Holy Spirit and with deep conviction" (1 Thessalonians 1:5). The gospel we preach today must go forth in the power of the Holy Spirit and deep conviction.

> When we pray, we receive the Holy Spirit. And when we pray, the Holy Spirit receives us.

When we pray, we receive the Holy Spirit. And when we pray, the Holy Spirit receives us. This is why prayer is so important. As we become surrendered and available to him, he anoints us to present Jesus in all his fullness to a dying world. Prayer evangelism as an ongoing force in the local church keeps this dynamic alive in the evangelistic efforts of the church.

This relationship between prayer and the Holy Spirit is illustrated in Luke 3:31: "And as he was praying, heaven was opened and the Holy Spirit descended on him...." As Jesus prayed, he received the Holy Spirit. Then in the next chapter we read, "Jesus returned to Galilee in the power of the Spirit"(Luke 4:14). In Luke 4:18 he said, "The Spirit of the Lord is on me, because he has anointed me to preach the good news to the poor." In Luke 5:16, we read, "But Jesus often withdrew to lonely places and prayed" and in the next verse, "And the power of the Lord was present for him to heal the sick." In Luke 6:12 he spent the whole night praying. Luke 6:19 says, "and the people all tried to touch him, because power was coming from him and healing them all." When Jesus prayed, he received the Spirit's power.

> We pray, and the Spirit comes; we pray and surrender, and he uses us in a new way.

Jesus summed up his teaching with these words, "If you then, though you are evil, know how to give good gifts to your children, how much more will your Father in heaven give the Holy Spirit to those who ask him!" (Luke 11:13). In Luke 24:49 Jesus tells them, "I am going to send you what my Father has promised, but stay in the city until you have been clothed with power on high."

Inhaling the Breath of God

When we pray, we receive the Holy Spirit. This reception may be felt or unfelt—it does not matter. What matters is that we believe he has come and made us ready to serve him. In Acts 1:14 they prayed, and in Acts 2 the Holy Spirit came upon them. In Acts 4:31 they prayed, and the Evangelist came. A Christian's initial infilling is important, but subsequent infillings are just as important if we are to evangelize our cities. In Acts 8:15 "they prayed for them that they might receive the Holy Spirit." In dramatic moments and in quite less dramatic moments the Spirit comes in answer to prayer. In John 20:21-22, Jesus said to them, "'As the Father has sent me, I am sending you.' And with that he breathed on them and said, 'Receive the Holy Spirit.'" When we pray he breathes upon us. Prayer is to inhale the breath of God. Evangelism is exhaling what we inhale in prayer.

Further, when we pray we surrender to him for him to use us. Corporate prayer renders the church available to him. In Acts 1:14 the church prayed and became available to witness in Jerusalem. In Acts 3 Peter and John went to pray and became available to heal a man crippled from birth. In Acts 8 Philip became available to Samaria and later in the chapter he was available to be used to win the Ethiopian. In Acts 9 Ananias became available to pray for Saul. In Acts 10 Peter was praying on the roof and became available to reach Cornelius and thereby open a door for communicating the gospel to the Gentiles.

We pray, and the Spirit comes; we pray and surrender, and he uses us in a new way. The format in the book of Acts is simple: they prayed, he came, they evangelized. What was the result? Acts 16:5 records the answer: "The churches were strengthened in the faith and grew daily in numbers."

Notes

A Power Greater than Advertising

The church today needs the work of this Holy Evangelist. There are as many church growth plans as there are churches. There are as many good ideas as there are people to do them. And pastors often lament that their church needs a better location or a brighter sign or more advertising. But, what we need is power, holy unction from on high to win the lost, and this anointing comes in answer to prayer. Churches that are praying in greater ways are finding this so. Paul Cho tells of when he met the Holy Spirit as Evangelist:

> I tried hard to lead people to Christ, but with few results. As I was in prayer, the Lord spoke to my heart, "How many quail would Israel have caught if they had gone quail hunting in the wilderness?" I responded, "Lord not too many." "How did the quail get caught?" the Lord continued to ask me. I then realized that God sent the wind which brought the quail. The Lord was trying to show me the difference between chasing souls without the Holy Spirit's strategy and working in co-operation with the Holy Spirit. Then the Lord said something to me that totally changed my life, "You must get to know and work with the Holy Spirit!" I knew I was born again. I knew I was filled with the Holy Spirit. Yet, I had always thought of the Holy Spirit as an experience and not as a personality."[3]

Paul Cho now pastors the largest church in the world with over 700,000 members. The Holy Spirit has certainly "blown" many souls into his church camp!

Good church growth principles are important, but more important is the work of the Holy Spirit in them. Prayer evangelism bridges the gap between technique and anointing. A prayer room can serve as the vehicle for prayer evangelism in your church when it has as its focus a vision of reaching the lost. Such praying can carry out the Great Commission in the local church in several ways.

During Desert Storm a major portion of the air attack was directed by high flying radar command posts called AWACs that overlooked the entire theater of operation. Satellites, even higher, would take pictures of enemy targets and relay the information to the AWAC command post. From here orders were given for the air attack that fell on enemy targets with pinpoint accuracy. This precision attack was guided by the all-seeing battle control centers that hovered high above from a lofty vantage point.

> As we pray over the city, the Holy Spirit guides the attack to win the lost.

I believe a prayer center serves in much the same way. As we pray over the church, the city and the world, the Holy Spirit guides the attack to win the lost. As people come to a prayer center and call out to God using a county or city map or world globe, the Holy Spirit goes to work targeting areas that are ready for harvest. As people come to pray for different groups of people in the community and pray over lists of prospects, the work of the Spirit is felt in the church and the

Notes

community. The Holy Spirit touches the church in a powerful way to evangelize, and he works in the community preparing people for the message and salvation.

Eight Ways the Holy Spirit Works in the Church

The sustained effort of prayer-evangelism in a prayer center attracts the Holy Spirit to do at least eight important things in a church in order for it to evangelize its community.

1. The Holy Spirit imparts compassion. As we pray, the Holy Spirit imparts this compassion for the lost. Paul had such a burden. He writes in Romans 10:1, "Brothers, my heart's desire and prayer to God for the Israelites is that they may be saved." Earlier in Romans 9:1-4 he declares that if possible he would forfeit his own place in Christ if they could be saved. What a burden!

When people come to pray and cry over the local schools in a prayer room, a burden is imparted for the salvation of our youth. The Spirit motivates evangelism by giving a burden for lost men, women, and children. As we pray, the love of God for a lost world is poured out in our hearts (Romans 5:5). He is the agent of love. As we pray, the Holy Spirit imparts the love that transcends technique; he overcomes our apathy and coldness of heart; he moves us to the self-sacrifice required to build a relationship with a lost person to secure them in Christ.

2. The Holy Spirit calls us to repentance. Repentance begins with the church first and then spreads outside to the city. List the sins of the church and the sins of your city. As intercessors pray in the prayer room, corporate repentance takes place as a work of the Spirit. Second Chronicles 7:14 states,

> *... If my people, who are called by my name, will humble themselves and pray and seek my face and turn from their wicked ways, then I will*

*hear from heaven and will forgive their sin and
will heal their land.*

John Dawson suggests in his book *Taking Our Cities for God*, that research can be done to discover the history of a city's sinfulness and its original Christian roots.[4] If possible, name its sins—pride, rebellion, immorality, prejudice. As sins are dealt with in the church and the city, God will pour out his Spirit for evangelistic success. As evil spiritual powers are driven back, the gospel will go forth unhindered.

3. The Holy Spirit guides our outreach and gives us a relevant message for our community. Jesus said, "When the Counselor comes, whom I will send to you from the Father, the Spirit of truth who goes out from the Father, he will testify about me, but you also must testify..." (John 15:26-27). You may be led to prayer room intercession over the country club, yielding a witness to that set of people. One church prays fervently in its prayer room for its addicted populations. The same church was led to start Christian Twelve Step groups for people with co-dependent and addictive behaviors. Jesus meets people at the point of their personal need, as the Holy Evangelist leads the church in this ministry.

When a church prays continually in a corporate manner over its

vision and outreach, the Spirit initiates mission. In Acts the Spirit sent Philip down to Samaria. In obedience to the Spirit he went and stood by the desert road to Gaza and won an Ethiopian to the Lord. Ananias was led to Judas' house on Straight Street, and there he found Saul, later to become Paul. Peter was guided to Cornelius' house and a door to the Gentiles was opened. Time after time the Holy Spirit directed the early church's outreach.

> "Indeed, love is about the only power in the world which is stronger than fear."

No wonder Paul asked, "And pray for us, too, that God may open a door for our message...." (Colossians 4:3). We know that not everyone is open to the gospel at any time, yet there are people in a city who are receptive to the gospel. The Spirit leads those in the church who are ready to tell to those who are ready to hear. This divine alignment in evangelism is the work of the Holy Spirit in answer to prayer.

4. The Spirit empowers Christians for witness. Jesus said, "But you will receive power when the Holy Spirit comes on you; and you will be my witnesses in Jerusalem, and in all Judea and Samaria, and to the ends of the earth" (Acts 1:8). The Holy Spirit comes to anoint the church's witness. Michael Green writes,

> *He can give the power we need, and only he. Power for being witness to Jesus—is that not needed? Are not many Christians tongue-tied at the thought of speaking to anyone else about their Lord, while others find it second nature? The difference lies in the Holy Spirit, and whether or not he has been asked to take over. Power to cast out fear—is that not needed? Are many Christians not only speechless about Jesus, but crippled by fear and inhibitions about launching out in the service of the good news? The perfect love which the Spirit gives casts out fear. Indeed,*

love is about the only power in the world which is stronger than fear.... I have no doubt that Peter was terrified when he found himself in the earliest days of the church dragged before a full meeting of the Jewish Sanhedrin, with all the hatchetmen of the high priest's family gathered with them, to defend his preaching and healing in the name of the man they had all hated enough to crucify. A very threatening situation. But we read that "Peter, filled with the Holy Spirit, said to them..." (Acts 4:8). The love and power of the Spirit cast out his natural fear. And if you ask the Spirit to fill you, he will do the same for you."[5]

All across the country men and women are praying in the prayer room during the worship service. They pray for the pastor to boldly proclaim the message and for the word to achieve that for which it was sent. They pray in the prayer room for visitation teams to have divine appointments to share Christ and for the Holy Spirit to empower them to speak the right words at the right time.

5. The Holy Spirit grants laborers for the harvest. Jesus said, "the harvest is plentiful, but the workers are few. Ask the Lord of the harvest, therefore, to send out workers into his harvest field" (Matthew 9:37-38). In Acts 6:4 they gave themselves to pray for laborers. Then came Stephen, Philip, Procorus, Nicanor, Timon, Parmenas and Nicolas. The Holy Spirit brings youth workers, children's workers, telephone workers and others to labor in the church's harvest fields. Ask and they will be given—teachers, givers, volunteers, encouragers. He will raise them up or move them in to join the church and work for the harvest—all in answer to corporate prayer offered up in the prayer room.

One of the most successful ministries in the world is Campus Crusade for Christ. This ministry was begun by a layman, Bill Bright. They have laborers sharing on thousands of campuses around the world. They believe prayer accesses the source for these laborers. In the late 1960s they started a prayer room in their headquarters in Arrowhead Springs, near San Bernardino, California. Intercessors pray on a full-time basis (i.e., currently, there are 10 prayer warriors each praying 40 hours a week) in their prayer chapel. These intercessors raise their own support as "prayer missionaries." They receive prayer requests by telephone (1-714-883-0734). As well, they pray for the Campus Crusade outreaches around the world.

They are now opening a second prayer center in Orlando, Florida, called the "War Room." This room will have large bulletin boards with information to pray for concerns around the world. Bill Jennings is the coordinator of their prayers. He believes that Campus Crusade is a testimony to the principle that the Holy Spirit supplies the workers when we pray.

6. The Spirit gives means and resourceful ideas to the church's outreach. He is the Holy Spirit of creative ideas for reaching cities for Christ. New methods and approaches to evangelism are the work of the Spirit. Set before the intercessors this prayer: "Lord of creation, what will it take to reach our city for you? Show us some new, simple, specific ways to be fruitful for you in this city. Amen."

A church in Texas, which has a dynamic worship ministry, prayed this prayer. As a result they began to record special services of only praise and worship, duplicate the tapes, and design a first-class cover for them. These tapes were then distributed, several hundred at a time, door-to-door in unchurched neighborhoods in their city. That is one example of creative evangelism in answer to prayer.

7. The Spirit adds vitality and life to existing ministries in the local church. The Spirit empowers the life of the local church to make it attractive. Someone once said that a church must be worth joining before it can grow. A restaurant can have a good location and a great advertising campaign, but if the food is poor those who come to eat will not want to join the restaurant's clientele.

All the ministries of a local church affect its outreach to that city. Each needs to be the target of ongoing prayer: all aspects of worship—the music, the preaching, the invitation, the offering, Sunday School classes, youth ministry, and so forth. Prayer is essential.

Also, churches that are internally torn by divisions will not offer a bright light to their cities. Overall excitement and warmth in a church's fellowship is essential for growth and discipleship. Michael Green says,

> *Many churches are divided in theological emphasis, in social concerns, by personality cult, by jealousy, by unburied hatchets between church members, by harsh critical judgments on others.*

Notes

Who can impart love? Who can restore unity?
Only the Holy Spirit, if he is allowed to sweep in
cleansing power into the situation. It is only when
we come with our differences and together lay
them before the Lord in penitence and ask for
his Spirit to bind us together in love—it is only
then that the church can get the power to live
out its gospel.[6]

Corporate intercession over a church's membership can invite the Holy Spirit to clean house of any and all attitudes that diminish our witness for Christ. The Holy Spirit inspires the church to be the church of Jesus Christ, full of love and revealing the life of God.

> The primary work of the Holy Spirit is to make Jesus attractive to the unbelievers.

8. In answer to prayer the Spirit will give unity and a city-wide vision for the harvest. Churches are realizing that if we are to turn the tide of evil and reach our cities for Christ, we are going to have to cooperate. Isolated efforts will not greatly dent rising crime rates and drug traffic. Churches must pray together and combine hearts, minds and faith to take our cities for Christ.

Such prayer can begin in a local church prayer center where we repent of denominational pride, parochialism and competition that stands between churches. The Spirit bids us to list the churches in our community to pray over them. When they prosper, we prosper. A strong church must reach out to weak churches. Jesus prayed, "May they be brought to complete unity to let the world know that you sent me and have loved them even as you have loved me" (John 17:23). Twenth-four hour intercession for no other reason but this one request for unity would be well worth the effort.

In summary, prayer evangelism as seen in a prayer center on a corporate or personal level can empower the church to be effective in leading people to Christ. These eight are only a few of the significant ways that the Spirit can change and catapult a church into a lost neighborhood. It was said of Desert Storm, "the air war won the ground war." The fervent, faithful praying of a few in a well-developed prayer center can win the ground war for the troops of Christians going out into their places of work and neighborhoods to bear witness to Jesus Christ.

Ten Ways the Holy Spirit Works in the Unbeliever

The Holy Spirit works in the unbeliever in answer to prayer to bring that person to a saving faith in Jesus Christ. In fact, Paul states in 1 Corinthians 12:3, "... no one can say, 'Jesus is Lord,' except by the Holy Spirit." A public profession of Jesus Christ is the result of the Holy Spirit's work. Jesus said, "When the Counselor comes, whom I will send to you from the Father, the Spirit of truth who goes out from the Father, he will testify about me" (John 15:26).

The primary work of the Holy Spirit is to make Jesus attractive to the unbelievers. He illuminates the word of Jesus. He reveals the work of Jesus on the cross. He conveys the very love of Jesus for the sinner. He exposes the depth and width of Jesus' forgiveness. He details the beauty of the Son of God. The Spirit has come to show the

Notes

world how profound Jesus Christ is in all his attributes. And when unsaved people see Jesus in all his exaltation, they are compelled to either accept or reject him. One thing is sure, he cannot be ignored. This Jesus, as portrayed by the Spirit, transcends any religious or denominational caricature of him. When we pray, the Spirit goes to work to reveal Jesus to an unredeemed world. I believe his work is tenfold in the unbeliever.

1. The Spirit works to initially woo or draw someone to Jesus. He makes their heart hungry for the truth and ready to accept what Jesus has to offer. Jesus said, "No one can come to me unless the Father who sent me draws him" (John 6:44). In answer to prayer, the Spirit draws and prepares a person to accept Jesus. This wooing may take days, weeks or years, yet it is the preparation necessary prior to personal salvation.

Dick Eastman, author of several books on prayer, has a prayer center in his backyard. It is a one-room, carpeted prayer room that has world maps, names of leaders, prayer requests and various other prayer helps. He and his wife pray often in this room. He is zealous to pray for the unsaved nations like China.

In his book, *The Hour That Changes The World,* he encourages believers to pray that the unsaved Chinese would be plagued with these questions: "Whom can I trust? What is my purpose for living? When will I really be free? How can I cope with my problems? Where will I go when I die?"[7] As we know, Jesus is the answer to all these questions! But first, these questions must be asked to produce real discontentment in a heart. The work of the Spirit is to put these questions and many more like them before the unbeliever to set the stage for their conversion. The Spirit makes men and women thirsty for the living water.

2. The Spirit sends an anointed witness to testify to the unbeliever about Jesus. He sends someone to present "the message" in person.

In the book of Acts it was "the Word" or message about Jesus—his life, death and resurrection. The Spirit sent Peter on the day of Pentecost to bear witness; he sent Philip to the Ethiopian in Acts 8:26; he sent Ananias to Saul in Acts 9; he sent Peter to Cornelius in Acts 10. Romans 10:14-15 asks,

> *How, then can they call on the one they have not believed in? And how can they believe in the one of whom they have not heard? And how can they hear without someone preaching to them? And how can they preach unless they are sent?*

As it is written, "How beautiful are the feet of those who bring good news!"

The Spirit's work is to anoint and send witnesses to tell unsaved people about Jesus. When we pray, he may even send us!

3. John 16:8 says "When he comes, he will convict the world of guilt in regard to sin and righteousness and judgment." The Spirit works in the heart to show us how much we need Jesus. He shows us the horror of our empty hearts and lives. He makes it clear that our righteous deeds will not make us right with God. He puts a holy alarm in us that without Jesus there is no hope. This is the work of conviction. Acts 2:37 states, "When the people heard this (the word

about Jesus), they were cut to the heart and said to Peter and the other apostles, 'Brothers, what shall we do?'" One translation says "they were stung to the heart," another "stabbed to the heart," and one says "they were pierced to the heart." This is the work of the Spirit.

> Until we see the ugliness of our hearts, we cannot see the awesome beauty of Jesus.

Unless we are convicted at some point, we will not repent and turn to Jesus. Until we see the ugliness of our hearts, we cannot see the awesome beauty of Jesus. Until we see the sin sickness of our heart, we will not seek and accept him as the remedy for all sin. Perhaps this is why so many are "convicted" and pray to receive Christ in Reinhard Bonnke's meetings in Africa. The fervent prayer in the prayer tent allows the Spirit to work in those who hear the gospel. We must see our need for Jesus before we can accept him as Savior.

4. The Spirit also works to convince the unbeliever. We must never underestimate the power of doubt in the unbeliever. Paul writes,

> *But their minds were made dull, for to this day the same veil remains when the old covenant is read. It has not been removed, because only in Christ is it taken away.... And even if our gospel is veiled, it is veiled to those who are perishing. The god of this age has blinded the minds of unbelievers, so that they cannot see the light of the gospel of the glory of Christ, who is the image of God (2 Corinthians 3:14, 4:3-4).*

The veil of doubt can only be torn through much prayer in spiritual warfare for the person veiled by doubt and Satan.

The Holy Spirit works to free the unbeliever to see the light of the gospel in the face of Christ (2 Corinthians 4:6). He is the agent of faith overcoming their doubt. For example, the Spirit will work signs and wonders to convince the unbeliever of the reality of God and his love. In John 14:12 Jesus told us that we will do the same works he did. In Acts the apostles did heal the sick, raise the dead and cast out demons: "When the crowds heard Philip and saw the miraculous signs he did, they all paid close attention to what he said. With shrieks, evil spirits came out of many, and many paralytics and cripples were healed. So there was great joy in that city" (Acts 8:6-8). This is the convincing work of the Holy Spirit to cause belief in a city.

> "The gifts are not confined to the church services, they are tools employed in reaching the lost."

A good example of this work can be seen in the Vineyard Christian Fellowship movement headed by the late John Wimber. This new movement is greatly committed to collective prayer, and as a result, they see many signs and wonders in evangelism. John Wimber's books, *Power Healing* and *Power Evangelism*, explain the role of the Spirit in doing signs and wonders in evangelism. He writes,

> *Today we see hundreds of people healed every month in Vineyard Christian Fellowship services. Many more are healed as we pray for them in hospitals, on the streets, and in homes. The blind*

Notes

see, the lame walk, the deaf hear. Cancer is disappearing. Most importantly for me as a pastor, the people are taking healing and other supernatural gifts to the streets, leading many to Christ who otherwise would not be open to the message of the gospel of Christ. I estimate that twenty percent of our people regularly see someone healed through their prayers. The gifts are not confined to the church services, they are tools employed in reaching the lost.[8]

The Spirit works to overcome doubt in the unbeliever. He works to set them free from Satan and he enables them to believe on the strong Son of God, Jesus Christ. In a society like ours we need prayer centers to pull down the strongholds of rationalism, intellectualism and religious traditions (2 Corinthians 10:4-5). The writer of Hebrews aptly states, "God also testified to it (the message of Christ) by signs, wonders and various miracles, and gifts of the Holy Spirit distributed according to his will" (Hebrews 2:4).

> "I was driving by the church and something told me to come in here and ask you how I could get saved."

5. The Spirit opens the heart of the unbeliever to believe on Christ. Again, no one can confess "Jesus is Lord" without the Spirit. Jesus said, "This is why I told you that no one can come to me unless the Father has enabled him" (John 6:65). In Acts 16 we see an example of prayer and evangelism. We read,

On the Sabbath we went outside the city gate to the river, where we expected to find a place of prayer. We sat down and began to speak to the women who had gathered there. One of those listening was a woman named Lydia, a dealer in purple cloth from the city of Thyatira, who was a worshiper of God. The Lord opened her heart to respond to Paul's message (Acts 16:13-14).

Then Lydia and her household were baptized.

One pastor, Thomas Elliff, decided to spend his entire morning in prayer—no coffee break, no telephone, no meetings—just prayer. He writes,

> *At noon I opened the door to my study. I discovered a stranger waiting to visit for just a moment. "Pastor," he said. "You don't know me. I was driving by the church and something told me to come in here and ask you how I could get saved." In a matter of minutes he was born into God's family.*[9]

Elliff relates that this happened in a similar manner the next two days when he opened his study at noon. In the next two weeks over 100 individuals came forward during the invitation time, and half of them wanted to profess faith in Christ as Lord and Savior.

As we pray, the Spirit woos and opens hearts to believe. As the church Evangelist, the Spirit makes Jesus real to the unsaved community. Imagine you are a pastor trying to present Christ. Imagine the difference it would make to know that people are in a prayer center praying as you preach for minds all over the sanctuary to be opened to Christ for the first time!

6. The Holy Spirit is the Spirit of regeneration. In this process of salvation a hunger for God can occur, the word about Jesus can be presented, conviction may come along with a certainty to believe—yet without rebirth there can be no salvation. The Holy Spirit changes the unbeliever. He imparts the life of Jesus in us when we believe.

> *At one time we all were foolish, disobedient, deceived and enslaved by all kinds of passions and pleasures. We lived in malice and envy, being hated and hating one another. But when the kindness and love of God our Savior appeared, he saved us, not because of righteous things we had done, but because of his mercy. He saved us through the washing of rebirth and renewal by the Holy Spirit, whom he poured out on us generously through Jesus Christ our Savior...(Titus 3:3-6).*

He conforms us to the image of God in Christ Jesus. He puts the mind of Christ in us. He cleanses us of all sin. He makes us new. When does this happen? This work of the Spirit happens when we trust Christ and accept him as our Lord and Savior. Peter explains, "Repent and be baptized, everyone of you, in the name of Jesus Christ so that your sins may be forgiven. And you will receive the gift of the Holy Spirit" (Acts 2:38). The Spirit fills us with Jesus! The "sinner's prayer" is our initial step toward surrendering to the Holy Spirit for his life-changing work in us.

7. The Holy Spirit seals us in Christ when we accept him. Paul shares,

> *And you also were included in Christ when you heard the word of truth, the gospel of your salvation. Having believed, you were marked in him with the seal, the promised Holy Spirit, who is a deposit guaranteeing our inheritance until the redemption of those who are God's possession— to the praise of his glory (Ephesians 1:13-14).*

He secures us in Christ as the Father's very own workmanship. We are his. We bear his identity—it is clear. We are born from above. The Spirit is the "earnest" or "down payment" or "first installment" of what is to come in glory. The Spirit is our pledge of glory given to us when we believe. We pray earnestly for this to happen in the unbeliever.

8. The Spirit grants assurance to the new believer. Romans 8:16 accounts, "The Spirit himself testifies with our spirit that we are God's children." Being confident of our salvation is the work of the Spirit. Doubts are dispelled, assurance is given, peace with God is confirmed by the Holy Spirit. When someone is saved they will "know that they know."

In the prayer center of the church I once pastored they have a list of all the church members. The intercessors pray over each name, lifting that person up to God. The desire is that everyone in the church will know without a doubt that Jesus Christ lives in them.

We are made holy in him. He sanctifies or "sets us apart" in Christ Jesus. We are saved from sin to become like Jesus. Francis Frangipane says it well,

Our goal as church leaders and intercessors is

to abide in Jesus, not to elevate one denomination above another. John taught, "the one who says he abides in Him ought himself walk in the same manner as He walked" (1 John 2:6).... We must want Christ's image alone established in our hearts.... Therefore, the Father's goal, which must become our goal, is nothing less than Christlikeness, where we become fully trained in the knowledge of the ways of God. The Lord calls us to pay the same price, do the same works and possess the same benefits from prayer that Jesus did. We cannot afford to compromise what God has promised, nor disobey what he requires.[10]

Therefore, the corporate prayer of a prayer center is for Christlikeness in the church. We want the Holy Spirit to paint a picture of Jesus in us to unveil to the city, so as to attract people to him. Our prayer is, "Let our city see Jesus in his fullness." The Spirit works in us to display his kingdom traits.

> The goal of evangelism is not to make decisions, but to make disciples.

9. The Spirit develops the character of Jesus in the new believer. He reveals Jesus to conform us to Jesus. We call this the fruit of the Spirit. Galatians 5:22 describes Jesus, "But the fruit of the Spirit is love, joy, peace, patience, kindness, goodness, faithfulness, gentleness and self-control." Salvation in the New Testament has three tenses: we are saved, we are being saved, and we will be saved. The Spirit works in us continually making us like Jesus.

10. The Spirit works to incorporate people into the Body of Christ. Salvation is not just a personal experience. People are saved to become a part of the local church. We read, "And the Lord added to their number daily those who were being saved" (Acts 2:47). Again, "Nevertheless, more and more men and women believed in the Lord and were added to their number" (Acts 5:14). In Acts 9:31 we read, "Then the church throughout Judea, Galilee and Samaria enjoyed a time of peace. It was strengthened and encouraged by the Holy Spirit, it grew in numbers, living in the fear of the Lord."

The Holy Spirit is the church's Evangelist. As we pray he "joins" new converts to the local church. Here they find the fellowship of Jesus, teaching about Jesus and opportunities to serve Jesus. The Spirit works to surround new Christians in a supportive atmosphere so they can grow and be nurtured. He brings them to a church where they can worship and pray. The goal of evangelism is not to make decisions, but to make disciples.

Working Both Sides of the Stained Glass Curtain

In summary, the Holy Spirit does the work of evangelism. As we pray, he comes to anoint and appoint us to the task of winning our cities to God. He works in the church and in the lost city to bring about salvation. D. Martyn Lloyd-Jones says in his book *Joy Unspeakable,*[11] "Go through Acts and in every instance when we are told either that the Spirit came upon these men or that they were filled

Notes

with the Spirit, you will find that it was in order to bear witness and a testimony." Acts 4:33 says, "With great power the apostles continued to testify to the resurrection of the Lord Jesus, and much grace was with them all."

Prayer evangelism stirs the Spirit in the church to be excited about Jesus and sharing Jesus with the world. He also stirs the city to be hungry for the message of the gospel to receive the truth about Jesus. Both of these works are essential to effective church growth.

If this is true, why not make room to pray? Why not set up a room to pray? Establish a place for prayer, or revive your current room with a vision for the city. In the following chapters I offer some practical ideas on how to make room to pray. These ideas come from a variety of churches and ministries that have made room to pray and are quite successful at it. Michael Green sums it up.

> *How much we need the Holy Spirit in our church life! Had it struck you that if the New Testament is right in the marrying up of the Holy Spirit with witness bearing, this might shed a flood of light on the poverty of spiritual experience in many a church and many a Christian? Could it be that we know so little of the Spirit in any powerful way because we care so little for evangelism? Equally, that we know so little of the Spirit? These two God has joined together, and we cannot put them asunder. No evangelism, no Holy Spirit; no Holy Spirit, no evangelism. There is a vital link between them, and that explains a good deal of the powerlessness in the modern church. The early Christians were well aware that the Holy Spirit and evangelism went together and affected each other intimately.[12]*

Therefore, let us not resist, nor quench, nor grieve, nor fear, nor despise this Holy Spirit, but welcome him on our knees to reveal Jesus in all his radiant fullness.

Brainstorm

What are your church's three most important ministries to reach people with the gospel message?

1.

2.

3.

Are there areas of tension or factionalism that would harm the witness of your church?

Chapter Four

Persuading Leaders to Make Room to Pray

It is interesting that we spend thousands of dollars on sanctuaries and family life centers and yet spend so little to create places to pray in these buildings. We plan elaborate structures with everyone in mind—youth, children, singles, persons with disabilities—yet we provide no space for continued or occasional prayer. We have music rooms for sheet music and robes, but no place to pray. We have a parlor for the bride, but no room to wait on the coming of the Groom of Glory. We have a room for youth recreation, but no place for prayer re-creation. We say people could pray in the sanctuary, but for security reasons it is locked up. Besides, to turn the air conditioning on would cost too much. We have room for everything and everybody, but no room to seek his face.

> We have room for everything and everybody, but no room to seek his face.

Yet Jesus said, "My house will be called a house of prayer" (Matthew 21:13). He was quoting Isaiah 56:7 where it states that the Father's house shall be called a house of prayer for all nations. Most churches do have an altar rail, but often it is rarely used except for communion. Some churches may once have had a place for prayer, but now it is rarely used, and the Christmas decorations are stored there. And with little place to pray, prayer may have little place in the hearts of the congregation.

Let me ask you, would you have a prayer center in your local church? Would you like to have a prayer center that is inviting, inspirational and informational? Could you envision corporate prayer as an ongoing force in your church in order to take your city for God? Could prayer be ongoing in the life of your church rather than an occasional event for a crisis or a revival?

> We schedule worship, committee meetings and Sunday School, so why not prayer?

In this chapter, I begin explaining the "how to's" of installing a place for prayer in your church. Whereas the first three chapters dealt with the inspirational aspects of prayer, now I would like to focus on the perspirational steps necessary to making room for prayer. The concern in this chapter is how to begin.

Ten Reasons Why Your Church Needs a Prayer Center

Of course, as you read this you may be convinced or somewhat interested in making room to pray in your church, but first you need to persuade the pastor or trustees or current leadership that this is a good idea. To help you convince your leadership of the need for a prayer center, here are some additional advantages of a prayer room to add to those mentioned in Chapters Two and Three.

1. A prayer center makes it possible to schedule prayer in a systematic manner. There are four obstacles to intercessory prayer, two are spiritual and two are natural.

One, people do not pray because of sin. They don't want to get close to God when there is unconfessed sin in their life.

Two, people do not pray because of doubt. If we don't believe that prayer works, why pray? Mark 6:5-6 says, "He (Jesus) could not do any miracles there, except to lay hands on a few sick people and heal them. And he was amazed at their lack of faith." Doubt keeps us from praying. Unbelief promotes resignation and acceptance of the status quo. Mark Rutland, president of Southeastern Bible College, equates prayerlessness with atheism. In a sense, prayerlessness denies God's existence. When we do not pray, we are saying God is not able or is uncaring in this situation. Prayerlessness is a form of modern secular deism, the belief that God may have created the world, but he's off somewhere else and we are left to our own devices. So why pray? We might as well not tie up a room unnecessarily.

Three, people don't pray because they lack a prayer vocabulary. They do not know what to say to God, and they get tired of saying the same old thing.

Four, we do not pray, because we do not schedule it. We are so busy and so involved that prayer often gets squeezed out, and we don't make the time to pray. If we schedule prayer, we are more likely to pray because time is set aside to be with the Father. We schedule worship, committee meetings and Sunday School, so why not prayer?

A prayer room allows people to set aside a definite time to pray. In a 24-hour period they pick an hour and they can be held accountable to pray during that hour. By scheduling prayer, it is more likely to

Notes

happen. In the Book of Acts, there were stated hours of prayer. In Acts 2:15 it was nine p.m. In Acts 3:1 they went to pray "at three in the afternoon." Again in Acts 10:30, the hour was three. In Acts 10:9 there was prayer at noon. A place that is ready permits people to come at stated hours. If you make room to pray, you can schedule corporate prayer.

2. A prayer center provides a place to promote agreement in prayer. Jesus said, "Again, I tell you that if two of you on earth agree about anything you ask for, it will be done for you by my Father in heaven" (Matthew 18:19). By placing the city before your intercessors in the prayer room, everyone in there can be seeking God for the same thing—the salvation of your community. Systematically, you can present the vision of city-wide revival to your prayer warriors so they can soak the city in prayer. Maps, pictures and globes can visually motivate prayer. One church prays street-by-street. Another prayer room has nice pictures of the high schools, court house, police station and city hall for targeted prayer. Another church has prayer stations with lists of leaders, church goals, prospects for the kingdom and even a list of pregnant women in the church!

The prayer center in the Metro-Covenant Church in Dallas, Texas, arranges their prayer focus to pray for the surrounding cities in a unique manner. On the north wall of the center are the names of all the cities to the north, on the east wall, all the cities to the east, and so on. Intercessors stand and face these walls to pray for these cities, or they pray from given directions.

People who pray want to know what to pray about, and making a room to pray which contains pertinent information is helpful. Edwin Cole said, "Agreement produces strength and disagreement produces weakness."

3. A prayer center is a great place to register the deeds of God in the life of the church. The Bible says, "Enter his gates with thanksgiving and his courts with praise; give thanks to him and praise his name (Psalm 100:4). Also, "Praise the Lord, O my soul, and forget not all his benefits" (Psalm 103.2). Plus, "Who can proclaim the mighty works of the Lord or fully declare his praise?" (Psalm 106:2). We can remember and proclaim the acts of God if we write them down.

One of the oldest prayer rooms in America is at the Titusville Baptist Church in Titusville, Florida. They made room to pray in 1972. In their room they have a whole wall of notebooks that record the miracles of God since that year. Each notebook contains one month of answered prayers. They have 228 notebooks of answered prayer, and they now have to store some notebooks in boxes because they ran out of room. This recording of the deeds of God can produce a sense of praise and thanksgiving in the people who pray. Just as many Christians journal or record their requests and answers, a church needs its own journal to remember all that God has done! The prayer center is an ideal place for this registry. Make room to pray and remember what God has done, for to him and him alone belong glory.

> We can remember and proclaim the acts of God if we write them down.

4. Prayer centers promote ownership of the church vision.
One day as I was going into the church office, an old farmer came out of the prayer room. He had signed up to pray at noon on Tuesday. He wore his blue jeans and boots, and he had been praying for the church and city. He normally would only come to the church and plant flowers or attend Sunday morning worship, but here he was praying on Tuesday. In fact, we had 150 people signed up to pray. For many, this

is a new way of committing to the Lord's agenda for the city. Diversity in membership plus ownership of the city-wide vision equals a unity that yields a harvest for the kingdom.

What is also exciting is the fact that churches are synchronizing their prayer rooms in cities. Different churches are praying about the same thing: a city-wide spiritual awakening. The end result is the prosperity of all churches in town, declining crime rates and increasing holiness in the city. Churches praying in their respective rooms or places creates an ownership of God's vision for his church and for the city. For a more unified church, make room to pray.

5. Prayer centers give an advantage to evangelism by the image they cast in the community. As prayer is aimed at personal needs of unsaved people, they are touched by the compassion of Jesus. There is no higher expression of love than to pray for someone. As people in the city find out that your prayer room is a place of prayer for family crises, marriage problems, financial difficulties and other needs, they see you as a caring church. For them your prayer room is an emergency room to call when disaster strikes. And if people perceive you as a caring, praying, sharing congregation, they are more likely to attend your church. The Holy Spirit can use this positive image to draw people to Christ in your church. Pastors with prayer centers will tell you that this perceived image helps their churches grow. Make room to pray, and then make room for hurting people!

> Make room to pray, and then make room for hurting people!

One of the most active prayer rooms in America is the Upper Room in Nashville, Tennessee. This prayer center is sponsored by the United Methodist Church. Twenty-four hours a day they receive calls from hurting people all over the country who need prayer and love. If you ask the volunteers who work there, "Why?" they will answer, "Because we love people." When someone is hurting, there is no finer expression of Christ's love than to pray for them. Would that every church had the capability, compassion and availability to pray for hurting people in their community.

6. Prayer rooms provide a place for people to practice prayer. Someone got in a cab in New York City and asked, "How do you get to Carnegie Hall?" The cab driver turned and said, "Practice, man, practice!" The best way to learn prayer is to practice prayer. Prayer rooms are practice rooms. The Holy Spirit affects each intercessor and guides them in the quest of prayer. When the prayer center is used by groups, new converts hear seasoned saints pray, and they learn how to pray by listening to models of prayer. Thus, the prayer center is a training center for corporate and individual prayer. Intercession, like a lot of things, "is better caught than taught."

Jesus' disciples said, "Teach us to pray" (Luke 11:1). Parents can bring their children into a prayer room and let the children hear them pray for the city, church or someone in need. Children learn by example, and what better example than a kneeling dad or persevering mom in prayer. Some children who came with their parents to the prayer room asked their parents, "Why don't we have a room like this in our home?" So some of the parents went home to make a family altar or a prayer room in the home. One couple cleaned out their master bedroom closet and put in a nice "prayer closet." They say their little girl spends a lot of time in there praying instead of watching television. Make room to practice prayer, and perhaps your homes will be "altared."

Notes

7. Making room to pray can have an inclusive impact on your church. As stated in Chapter One, the Upper Room prayer center was made up of apostles, women, new converts, Jesus' own brothers and other seasoned saints. They represented different spiritual levels. They also came from all walks of life—fishermen, religious leaders, soldiers, ex-tax collectors and ex-beggars. They were of different educational levels. Some could read Hebrew, some could not. They were of different economic backgrounds. Some were cultured, others were uncultured. Yet, we read "they were in one accord."

This phrase "in one accord" (used in the King James translation), was used six times in the book of Acts (Acts 1:14, 2:1, 2:46, 4:24, 5:12, and 15:25). They were a diverse lot, yet they were in one accord in supplication, anticipation, continuation and adoration of Jesus. Prayer can unify people in many ways. Making room to pray can make people one in the Lord. The Holy Spirit helps us pray in agreement with the Father to glorify the Son. He makes us one. The prayer center brings new converts, seasoned saints, new members and old members to one place to pray. One pastor said he had people so shy they would not lead in silent prayer. A prayer room is a good place for anyone to pray, listen and learn the art of communicating with God.

> In our society, solitude is hard to come by, even in church!

8. A prayer room is a place where people can be quiet and hear the voice of God. In our society, solitude is hard to come by, even in church! Homes are inundated with noise, telephones, televisions and people. Jesus himself rose early to find a quiet place (Mark 1:35-37). We read, "Yet the news about him spread all the more, so that crowds of people came to hear him and to be healed of their sicknesses. But Jesus often withdrew to lonely places and prayed" (Luke 5:15-16).

As people pray, God speaks, and he guides the church. A prayer room might have twelve notebooks under the themes of praise, waiting, confession, scripture-praying, intercession, petition, singing, listening, meditation, watching, thanksgiving and praise. As people pray, they could record what they hear. Quite often from the most unlikely sources God speaks a word to the Church.

Prayer rooms provide a free, secure, comfortable place for people to be alone with God. He is speaking, and we must hear. The Lord speaks in Psalm 46:10, "Be still, and know that I am God." Collectively the church needs this stillness; make room to be still.

9. A prayer center provides a place for prolonged periods of prayer. Now I know it is not how long we pray that makes the difference; but, I do know that there are times when we need to travail in prayer. Sometimes five or ten minutes is enough, or even at times 30 or 40 minutes is needed. An hour of prayer is not out of the question. But, on rare occasions, the Lord may call a Christian or a church to a prolonged time of prayer to receive a needed breakthrough. A prayer center is conducive to this birthing type of prayer. The center is used only for prayer—no AA group is coming to meet, the nursery committee does not need the room, it is not subject to closure at 5:00. It is a place for whatever period of prayer is necessary.

The Upper Room Principle says we seek God until we receive an answer or a word. We wait until we know that we know that we know. We stay before him, presenting ourselves till he speaks. In 2 Chronicles 20, Israel came under severe attack. Jehoshaphat called a prayer meeting. He prayed, "For we have no power to face this vast army that is attacking us. We do not know what to do, but our eyes are upon you."

Notes

And then we read, "All the men of Judah, with their wives and children and little ones, stood before the Lord" (2 Chronicles 20:12-13).
How long did they stand there? We do not know. But I think they
stood there as long as they had to! They stood there until they under-
stood the answer clearly.

In a society that thrives on instant coffee, fast food and quick advice, we had better not lose our capac-
ity to wait on God. Having a place for

> In a society that thrives on
> instant coffee, fast food
> and quick advice, we had
> better not lose our capacity
> to wait on God.

prolonged, uninterrupted seeking is an
advantage we cannot do without. Make
room to stay before God if necessary. I
hate to think what might have happened if Jehoshaphat and his people had
bolted from waiting and done something
on their own. But they stood in place,
waiting, waiting, and then the answer came. The end result was that
the enemy was routed and victory prevailed.

**10. Prayer rooms can provide a quiet, private place when
needed by prayer counselors or church staff.** When we built our
church, we placed a prayer room right off the sanctuary so that people
could be taken there when they were upset or when they were making a commitment to Christ. It provides privacy for prayer and altar
counseling.

Church staff members can gather around a person and lay hands
on them and pray for healing. The staff can meet and pray together
before staff meetings or board meetings. Of course, the use of time in
the prayer room needs to be coordinated with those who have signed
up to pray for an hour. Nevertheless, a prayer room that is private,
quiet and worshipful provides a setting where commitments to Christ
or personal ministry can take place.

Gain Crucial Support

There are many advantages to having a prayer center in a local
church. The above suggestions should be helpful in persuading your
church leadership that the idea is a good one. However, one person's

support is crucial to the success of a prayer center—the pastor's. When a pastor has a vision for it, the prayer room thrives. But when he or she does not feel it is important, it will be hard to maintain.

When we visited the prayer room at First Baptist Church in Euless, Texas, the couple in the room at that time were quick to point out that Pastor Jimmy Draper and his wife pray in the room at 11 p.m. on Saturday night. They were encouraged that their pastor supported the intercessory prayer ministry by his participation. As a pastor, I found this to be true. When I preached on prayer from the pulpit to recruit intercessors for the prayer room, my participation made all the difference. When I held up answers to prayer on Sunday morning and we thanked God for answered prayer, the congregation was motivated to pray more.

The pastor's support is crucial to the success of a prayer center. Al Vander Griend writes,

> *A congregation will follow the example of its praying leaders. A strong prayer commitment on the part of your leaders will convey more to your congregation about the power and reality of prayer than seminars, articles, or special speakers.*[16]

Therefore, take time to gain the support of your pastor and church leadership when developing a prayer center. Give them this book, visit a couple of prayer rooms, have the prayer coordinator of another church talk to them. Take your time. Pray about timing and means as you approach leaders to gain their confidence and involvement. Give your pastor good books on prayer (See Resource List). Whatever it takes, get them to see the vision of a prayer center dedicated to intercessory prayer for the church and the city.

Brainstorm

Starting with the senior pastor, list the leadership of your church. Include laity that lead various groups.

How might you pass the vision for a prayer room on to those in leadership?

Chapter Five

Steps to Making Room to Pray

One of the most dynamic Baptist Student Centers in America is at Texas A&M University in College Station, Texas. Many students come to know Jesus Christ as Savior in this student center. At their noon Bible studies, close to 500 students crowd into a Fellowship Hall that seats 300! Their outreach to the campus of Texas A&M is extremely effective. Everything they do is blessed in spirit and numbers.

> They believe their success is due to this foundation of corporate, consistent intercession, so prayer is the most important thing they do.

If you ask Mike Graham, the Baptist Student Union Director, "Why?" he will answer, "Because we pray! We call our students to prayer. We divide the campus up and have students pray for specific dorms and academic buildings. They meet often for special corporate times of prayer for the campus and city."

At the core of their success is a prayer room in the B.S.U. Center. Because prayer is important, students sign up in pairs to pray for an hour. The room itself is planned to encourage intercessory prayer for personal needs and requests. They pray for missionaries and future outreaches to win people to Christ. This kind of prayer goes on from 8 a.m. to 5 p.m., Monday through Friday. They believe their success is due to this foundation of corporate, consistent intercession, so prayer is the most important thing they do. They put a lot of work into developing their prayer ministries. They have a plan, prayer leaders, training, recruitment and ways of expressing appreciation for their prayer workers. The staff of the B.S.U. believes that a high degree of quality is essential to a fruitful prayer ministry.

> What we put into a prayer room says something about prayer and its place in our ministry.

Tips for Organizing a Quality Prayer Room

What we put into a prayer room says something about prayer and its place in our ministry. Certain questions need to be asked. Is it clean? Is it neatly arranged? Is there quality furniture or carpet? Does it smell good? Is it accessible? Is it secure? Is it comfortable? I called one church and asked to see their prayer room. The secretary said, "Oh yes. We have a prayer room, but I don't know where it is. If you come over, we can find it for you!" Her lack of knowledge about where it was told me something.

When you go into the room, do you freeze or do you sweat as though you are in a sauna? If you kneel to pray, do you kneel in a puddle of milk from the Mother's Day Out program the day before? Or if you get on your face, do you smell chili in the carpet from the men's chili fund raiser? And are the prayer requests on the table dated September 1, 1945? Things like these tell you something about the importance of prayer. A place of prayer should, in appearance and essence, convey the supreme value of prayer in your church. Also, if you plan to start a prayer center, make plans to keep it going. Build into your plan a support base that will sustain the room for at least a year until it is established.

The following suggestions may help you to develop a prayer center for your church. Remember that no two churches are alike, therefore, your prayer center will be different. Plan and build according to your church size and membership make-up. Find a plan that will work for you.

1. Simply go to the Father and ask Him, "What kind of prayer center could we have?" "Where would it be?" Ask him to help you make a room to pray so that people can come and wait upon him. This may take some time, but the importance of the project demands it. Because Jesus said, "My house will be called a house of prayer" (Matthew 21:13), it is in the Father's heart to lead you in this endeavor. Trust him to provide favor with the pastor, elders, trustees, finance committee or whomever.

Our church began by recruiting people to pray at home. We did this for a year and a half, and it was time well spent when we got the actual room in place. Sow the seeds of the idea in your church. This gives the Father time to raise up the people necessary to make the dream come true.

2. Choose people to lead in the prayer room effort. A prayer committee can be made responsible for turning the idea into a functioning ministry in your church. Southern Baptist churches, like Central Baptist in Bryan, Texas, form committees on intercessory prayer

to develop the prayer room concept. Usually, six people serve on the committee to plan and do what is essential to establish the prayer room ministry. Of course the people on these committees have a vision for what prayer can become in their church and they are committed to seeing it happen. Time and prayer at this stage help locate the people with talents and gifts that can build a prayer force in the church.

A prayer room committee designs the initial stages of a prayer room's development. They can do several things to get the ball rolling. For example, they meet with the pastor to get his or her ideas, they develop a budget, determine location and prayer format, divide up assigned tasks like furnishing the room, recruitment, fund-raising, building and labor. Above all, their vision is to establish ongoing, informed intercessory prayer for the city. Prayer is the primary function of this place, so the design should serve the function. All plans for the prayer room need the approval of the church council or deacons, so the prayer committee needs to present the plans for final adoption. This creates more excitement and lay ownership of the ministry.

> Prayer is the primary function of this place, so the design should serve the function.

3. Develop a statement of purpose for the room. This purpose statement will be the definition for intercessory prayer in your prayer room. This helps keep the prayer committee on track as it builds and sustains the prayer room. Here is an example of a statement of purpose from Champion Forest Baptist Church:

PURPOSE

1. Provide a central place for maintaining and praying for the needs of individuals, the church, the nation and the world.

2. Provide an undergirding prayer support for all church endeavors and a source of power for ministry by the local church.

3. Lead the church in an understanding of and confidence in prayer.

4. Choose someone to lead or coordinate the ministry. Making room to pray consists of two basic stages. The initial stage is to build the room. This will be planned and managed by the prayer committee. The second stage is to actually see that the room functions. Most churches have a prayer room or prayer center coordinator to handle the daily operation of the room. This coordinator has the time to attend to all the details of making the room a fruitful place of prayer. A couple of sample job descriptions follow.

PRAYER MINISTRY DIRECTOR JOB DESCRIPTION

1. Oversee the intercessory prayer ministry.

2. Coordinate changes, programs and other activities with the church staff.

3. Keep pastor advised at all times.

4. Request pastor's counsel on significant matters.

5. Select and enlist prayer leadership.

6. Schedule prayer offering services and orientation and training meetings.

7. Schedule and conduct monthly leadership meetings.

8. Promote the Prayer Ministry throughout the church and community.

PRAYER COORDINATOR JOB DESCRIPTION

1. Oversee the prayer captains

■ Monitor attendance and encouragement program.

■ Assist prayer captains in solving problems; cover for them during their absence.

2. Be responsible for assigned prayer stations.

■ Keep information and materials current.

■ Review cards to remove outdated requests and record answers to prayer.

3. Suggest and implement improvements to the prayer ministry and the prayer room.

4. Train new prayer captains and intercessors.

5. Attend monthly leadership meetings.

5. Select a place in the church for the prayer center. We turned a storage room into our prayer room. You may want to use a Sunday School room at first. Some large churches build little white frame chapels in the front of the church. Others use a travel trailer pulled up next to the church. Whatever you choose, it important to meet city codes for building and fire protection.

Good lighting, heating and air-conditioning are essential. If possible, to conserve energy, the prayer room needs its own air and heating system, since it will be used all through the week.

Security is important, since people will be coming at night to pray. Most churches install security lights to flood the area leading up to the entrance. Some churches use a combination lock and the code is only given out to those who pray.

Accessibility to persons with handicaps is a major consideration. This would include a ramp, doorways wide enough for wheelchairs, appropriate table heights and parking for their cars.

An itemized budget would include all of the above items.

Furnish the room with quality furniture and decor. Money is easy to raise for a prayer room because people believe prayer is important. People like to give to certain things, especially things that are tangible, like buildings and pianos. They see these additions as lasting.

Once the prayer room is in place, the daily operations of the room should be put in the church budget. Again, design this place to fit your church's size and budget. If you have to, start small with a goal of enlarging the vision as you go. Suppose you develop a place and only two or three people a day come. That is a start, and it is two or three more than you had last year! Try to put quality into the room in every respect, from printed material to furnishings, because this says something about the importance of prayer.

6. Design a floor plan or format for your prayer room. The

floor plan of prayer rooms and centers should be conducive to prayer. By floor plan, I mean the pattern of prayer that will be used in the prayer room. This format may be simple with just a table, a card file for requests, a Bible and an answered prayer record keeping system. Or it may be more complex like the wall format in the Church on the Rock in Rockwall, Texas, with its hundreds of pictures and prayer items. Most prayer rooms use "stations" of prayer signifying various needs and subjects to be prayed over. People enter to prepare themselves, and then they move from station to station or go to a specific station to pray. One church uses library study carrels to give a sense of privacy for each station. This enables several to pray in the room at the same time.

The Vocabulary of Prayer

As mentioned in Chapter 4, vocabulary is important when it comes to prayer. Many people do not pray because they do not know what to say or pray for, and they cannot pray very long because they run out of words. Community needs are easy to pinpoint, but just praying for needs is depressing.

The help for vocabulary comes from the Bible. When we pray, we pray the Word of God! The Word provides his agenda for us to intercede for our city. Praying the scriptures makes corporate prayer come alive and saves it from boredom. If we study the Bible, why not pray the Bible? This is where prayer guides may be helpful.

> Praying the Scriptures makes corporate prayer come alive and saves it from boredom.

For example, the "Acts 29" prayer guide will help you claim the same works of the Holy Spirit that are described in Acts for your city. In other words, as you read Acts, ask God to do the same in your city. Of course there is no Acts 29, but since Acts 28 has no formal conclusion (because the Holy Spirit is not finished) we pray to write Acts 29 in our city. A variety of prayer guides are available, including the *Acts 29* prayer journey, or you may want to write one of your own.

A prayer guide simply leads prayer through the Word asking God to perform his Word in specific areas. Judson Cornwall's *Praying the Scriptures*[14] is a good textbook for this concept. Pray Psalm 91 as a protection over your churches. Pray through John 17 as you request unity for your city. Pray verses of the Bible like Matthew 11:28, "Lord bring the heavy laden to our church. Give the ease of your yoke," or "Lord you said in John 6:44 that no one can come to you unless the Father draws them. Please draw my neighbors as I name them before you." The Word of God gives vocabulary to prayer. The Word is the prayer language of the Father. Fill your prayer room with the Word. I will say more about the Word as a resource for prayer in the telephone training section.

The Pleasant Valley Baptist Church in Liberty, Missouri, attributes much of its growth and effectiveness to prayer. In their prayer room they have a one month of 24-hour prayer on a quarterly basis. The pastor prepares a prayer guide based on a theme that the church needs. Some of the Word-based themes have been developing friendships, developing self-esteem, finding your niche and dealing with stress. He isolates a need in the church, and then they soak it in prayer. In one month they will log 672 hours in prayer for that concern! They believe that this kind of prayer has made their church what it is today.

Notes

Deciding How to Pray

You may decide to arrange prayer stations to help people pray. This approach encourages variety and movement in the room for one or many people. This may include different postures like standing or kneeling, lying or sitting. Changing body position helps a person pray for an extended period of time.

> Changing body position helps a person pray for an extended period of time.

We used the Dick Eastman model based on his book *The Hour That Changes the World* (See Resource List). He simply took an hour and divided it into twelve five minute segments. This encourages people to pray for an hour in a systematic manner until they have formed good prayer habits. We had twelve prayer stations in our room. They were praise, waiting, confession, scripture praying, watching, intercession, petition, thanksgiving, singing, meditation, listening and praise.[15] Each station had a notebook with scriptures and concerns. For example, in the notebook on intercession, we had the names of our police force, pictures of city leaders, pictures of high schools, city hall, the county courthouse and the university. We had a list of church leaders and all the churches in our city. In the back of each notebook was additional space to write prayers, record reflections or revelations. In the thanksgiving notebook we recorded answers to prayer and all that we were thankful for. These stations were helpful, but we did not make them "the rule." People were also free to pray as they feel led. They may just kneel in front of the altar and wait on God, listening or giving thanks.

The good thing about these models is that there are books and tapes available to teach people how to pray in practical ways. For example, one summer I taught a chapter a week from Eastman's book. We developed a prayer journal, which our people used to intercede for the world and city. The journal had twelve sections and offered plans to record reflections and answers to prayer. I taught for twelve weeks on this prayer format. Then we used this format in our prayer room so that our people would have a place to practice what we taught them. We provided copies of the book in the room to be taken, so that there was an ongoing teaching of our format. This was very beneficial as a resource for our people so they knew what to do in the prayer room when they got there. Training builds confidence and expertise in prayer. Prayer is a discipline that can be learned and Eastman's model helps teach it. Also, by choosing a specific model, there is a sense of uniformity and consistency in prayer.

Highland Park UMC in Dallas, Texas has a Prayer Tower. The tower contains only a couch and a table with a Bible. The prayer room at Oral Roberts University, on the other hand, is quite complex and structured. Some churches use the format developed by Larry Lea based on the Lord's Prayer. Thousands of people use his guide to focus on the prayer Jesus taught his disciples in Matthew 6:9-13. The rooms may differ and the formats may differ, but the important thing is that people have a place and structure from which to pray.

Every church and ministry has to find what works best for them. These are only suggestions to stimulate creative thought. Find your mix, experiment, try a variety of approaches until you find what works best for your church.

Notes

Brainstorm

Think of names of people that would make good prayer room leaders. Don't overlook yourself.

Review the steps for starting a prayer room ministry. What step is your church on?

If you are in an organizing group, draft a statement of purpose.

Chapter Six

Recruiting People to Pray

Some may say, "This is all fine and good. I understand the benefits of a prayer room for our church and community. But our people don't pray." Pastors tell me, "I couldn't get people to come and pray. We have tried things like this before and they have been dismal failures. Our people just will not come to the church to pray." And to an extent, they are right. You can have a great prayer room, nice furniture, great format and wonderful location, but if people do not come to pray, your goal is not accomplished.

> God supports the idea of praying for lost people to be saved.

But we must remember that the Father's will is that all people be saved. Paul writes, "This is good, and pleases God our Savior, who wants all men to be saved and to come to the knowledge of the truth" (1 Timothy 2:3). John adds, "This is the assurance we have in approaching God: that if we ask anything according to his will, he hears us. And if we know that he hears us—whatever we ask—we know that we have what we asked of him" (1 John 5:14-15).

God supports the idea of praying for lost people to be saved. And if he supports the concept of prayer-evangelism, he will provide the vision, workers, resources and favor to get the job done. It is my conviction that he has already started a great prayer movement in the earth to win whole cities and nations unto himself. Therefore, your plans for a prayer center are right in line with what he is already doing. As Jack Taylor said, "Find out what God is doing, ask him if you can be a part of it, and you'll be blessed."

Tips for Prayer Room Recruitment

Some important principles can help you recruit people to pray. Here are a few to help you get started.

> Inspiring people to pray works better than using guilt to force people to pray.

1. The best place to recruit is from the pulpit. The most effective requests for prayer come from the pulpit on Sunday mornings. People support what the pastor holds up. And by preaching some messages on prayer, he or she can inspire people to sign up to pray in the prayer room.

One pastor challenged each person in his congregation to give one hour a week in the prayer center. He noted that ten percent of time would be seventeen hours a week, so one hour was not asking too much!

Inspiring people to pray works better than using guilt to force people to pray. Don't make people feel bad about not praying. Instead, let them see the prayer ministry as an opportunity to serve their Lord's vision for their city. Let the pastor sign up first, then the leadership, then the congregation.

2. Make sure your prayer room recruitment emphasis does not conflict with other major events in the church. Schedule for this event like you would your annual pledge campaign or revival.

3. Print the purpose of the prayer room in your bulletin or newsletter. Give updates on its development. One church put the names and pictures of the intercessory prayer committee members in the bulletin and stated what they were trying to do. Use the printed word as well as posters and even testimonies on Sunday morning to inspire people to sign up for one hour a week.

4. Approach groups in the church like the youth group, singles and women or men's groups. Make this a church-wide emphasis. Go to Sunday school classes and challenge them to take blocks of time. In one church the deacons took the hours on Sunday morning while the church worshiped.

> Walk all new members through the room as a part of new membership training.

5. Put a sign-up board in the foyer. Some set up a table in the foyer with a person to answer questions. The sign-up board works well because it is visual. You can buy one or make your own.

6. Make your prayer room part of the new member orientation. Walk all new members through the room as a part of new membership training. Encourage them to sign up as there are vacancies.

7. Emphasize special considerations that may help people feel more comfortable with the idea of signing up for prayer. For security reasons, we encouraged men to sign up for night hours

Notes

and women to sign up for day hours. Some women came in pairs during night hours. A one-way phone that intecessors can call out on is also a good idea. Schedule times that interested intecessors can tour the prayer room and have on-site training.

8. Use alternates and day captains to improve participation, insure round-the-clock praying and establish accountability. Ask people to sign up as alternates. If someone cannot come, they can call an alternate to fill in for them. Day captains can be responsible for each day's sign-up. A day captain serves as a coordinator of prayer for that day of the week. In other words, there is a Monday captain, Tuesday captain, etc. These captains help the prayer coordinator monitor daily attendance in the prayer room. Following is a typical job description for a day captain.

DAY CAPTAIN RESPONSIBILITIES

1. Pick up sign-in sheets each week and post attendance roster for group.

2. Call to encourage when:

■   Intercessor misses two weeks in a row (unless you have been notified of the reason ahead of time).

■   Attendance is sporadic over a long period of time.

■   You feel led to call those who are faithful or those you have not talked with in some time.

3. Work with the Sunday school class prayer leaders. Secure a list of class members scheduled each week to cover their assigned hour. Advise the class prayer leaders of attendance and absences so that proper accountability is maintained.

4. Check assigned prayer stations weekly to keep the prayer requests and other material updated and in proper order. Replenish supplies (pens, tissue, prayer note cards, etc.) as needed.

5. Work out problems where too many intercessors are scheduled during an hour and assist those who need to change their prayer time.

9. Have people sign up for a specific term of prayer. For example, sign them up to pray one hour a week, June through September. Term praying helps people schedule prayer during busy weeks. It helps them plan ahead to schedule themselves in the prayer room. And term praying helps them feel fulfilled when the term is over. They can say to themselves, "I did it. I prayed for four months in the prayer room." This develops prayer stamina. No one can run a mile or two without first conditioning themselves for the race. So it is with prayer. We must develop and condition ourselves to be consistent in prayer over a period of time. By getting in "prayer shape" we can commit to longer spans of time and be fulfilled. Teach your intercessors to recruit people to pray the next term. Ask them to ask their friends in the church. This encourages lay ownership of the ministry. Spread the load of recruitment to as many individuals as possible.

> By getting in "prayer shape" we can commit to longer spans of time and be fulfilled.

Notes

10. Publish the results of prayer in your church bulletin or newsletter or make prayer announcements from the pulpit. Answered prayer motivates prayer. One church started a 24-hour prayer ministry, and their giving skyrocketed. Everyone was excited. Our church saw a sharp increase in professions of faith as we started our prayer room ministry.

> Prayer requests should not be talked about outside the prayer room.

Remember, you may want to start small, perhaps with some weekend vigils of 30-minute intervals. It is helpful to set goals for recruitment. First United Methodist Church in Huntsville, Texas, set a goal of 40 hours per week. We set a goal of 144 (24 hours a day, six days a week, resting the prayer room ministry on Sunday.). The will and Word of God support the idea for a corporate prayer movement in your church. As we stated earlier, over 1,000 Southern Baptist Churches now have prayer rooms, and the number is growing daily. There is no divine reason why you cannot have a prayer center in your church staffed with faithful intercessors. Apply the Upper Room Principle—seek him and follow his leading.

Successful Prayer Room Training

After recruitment comes prayer room training. Tell people during the recruitment process that they will be trained. This offsets their fear of failure and the uncertainty of the unknown. If they know you will teach them what to do, they are more likely to sign up.

Your training plan will be dictated by the format you choose. If you adopt a prayer plan, teach intercessors how to use it. For instance, if you choose Eastman's model, make the textbook accessible. Some Baptist churches use the ACTS model. This stands for Adoration, Confession, Thanksgiving and Supplication. These are the four kinds of prayer used in the room. They teach this model and then use it in the room. Other resources are available to teach basic prayer methods. One is Maxie Dunham's book, *The Workbook of Living Prayer*.[16]

Then, teach your new recruits how to use the room. Review the basics of signing in, being on time and preparing to pray. You may offer these steps to help people prepare themselves to pray:

1. Get a Bible and pray according to his Word—1 John 5:14-15.

2. Pray in faith—James 5:15.

3. Realize you are to always pray, never giving up—Luke 18:1.

4. Come boldly into the throne room—Hebrews 4:16.

5. Plan to pray "in the name of Jesus"—John 16:23-24.

6. Know that God is hearing you—1 Peter 3:12.

7. Claim the power of earnest praying—James 5:16 (Amplified).

8. Recognize that power is released in prayer—Isaiah 55:11.

9. Recognize whom you are fighting—Ephesians 6:12.

Notes

10. Realize your power through Jesus over Satan—1 John 4:4.

11. Put on your prayer armor—Ephesians 6:13-17.

12. Purge yourself of uncleanness and unforgiveness— Matthew 18:21-35, Mark 11:25.

Emphasize the importance of confidentialty. Prayer requests should not be talked about outside the prayer room.

> A rule of thumb for most prayer ministries is that the greater the order, the more likely the ministry will last.

Show recruits how to write prayer-lines (a prayer line is a pre-printed note card with space to write a brief note of encouragement. It has the church name and address on it, and they are sent to those who are prayed for. These are a great encouragement to people who receive them. I had a member in a Dallas hospital who got six prayergrams from a church in Port Neches, Texas. He had never been to the church, nor did he know the people who sent them. Someone had simply turned his name in as a prayer request. He was blessed to know he was prayed for by a church he did not know!

Next, demonstrate how to systematically pray in the prayer center. Lead intercessors through a typical hour in the prayer room. Some churches provide a brief guide and overview to the prayer room ministry with rules and suggestions for prayer (See Resource List: *Prayer Room Intercessor's Handbook*).

If corporate prayer groups will use your prayer center at designated hours, train your leaders to lead these groups. Teach them to stick to the chosen agenda. Instruct them to take charge of the meeting, to begin on time and conclude on time. Give them permission to control people who pray too long or too loud or who distract the others from praying.

A rule of thumb for most prayer ministries is that the greater the order, the more likely the ministry will last. Corporate prayer ministries, whether using group or individual sign-up, need structure to keep them on track and focused. Without structure they tend to float around from need to need, or they follow the direction of a self-proclaimed leader.

Sometimes the enemy can ruin a good prayer ministry by planting a disruptive personality in the group to get it off track. Everyone who participates in corporate prayer needs to know the rules, guidelines and boundaries, and they must be willing to submit to the leadership of the group. Recall that the focus of this prayer is evangelistic. It is easy to get side-tracked by intercessors who, themselves, are hurting or in need of attention. Lovingly, these people must be expected to abide by the overall format to assure arrival at the destination: taking your city for God.

Every church is different; therefore, the actual training schedule will vary from place to place. One church dedicates the whole Sunday night program to training those who have signed up. They tell them what to do and what not to do in the prayer room. They simply go over the policies and procedures as noted above, things like arriving on time, who to call when you cannot come to pray, the procedure for praying the prayer requests and other general information. This kind of training focuses on the mechanics of the prayer room and assumes participants already have a rich personal prayer life. Intercessors are on their own as to how they will pray.

Notes

Another church has three sessions on Sunday afternoons at 4 p.m. to train people for the prayer room. Session one deals with prayer and resources on prayer. It teaches the chosen manner of prayer in the prayer center. Session two teaches the mechanics of the prayer room with an emphasis on prayer stations and what to do at each station. Session three gives examples of prayer covering a range of topics such as prayer for salvation, healing and spiritual warfare. Actual prayer is modeled before the trainees. Each session allows time for questions and answers. The sessions are recorded as teaching tools for any who cannot be in attendance. The training is led by the pastor and prayer room coordinator.

> People who are recruited as intercessors should be trained for prayer room intercession to ensure an effective prayer ministry.

Some churches offer little or no formal training. They simply sign people up to pray and leave instructions in the prayer room. However, I do not recommend this. People who are recruited as intercessors should be trained for prayer room intercession to ensure an effective prayer ministry. The training program can be developed by the prayer committee, prayer coordinator, pastor or a combination of those. There are many solid prayer resources that include prayer guides, prayer models and scripture prayers that are available for use in helping the intercessor stay focused and fresh for their time in the prayer room. (See Resource list: *Pray the Price Kit - Keys to the Kingdom*)

Obstacles to Corporate Prayer

All of the above may seem like a lot of work to have a prayer center ministry in your church. It is! You are looking at hours of preparation, planning and maintenance to keep it going. A vital, dynamic prayer ministry requires hard work.

Aside from this, several other reasons make it difficult to mobilize corporate prayer in the church.

1. The church has been inundated with what I call "Christian humanism." Humanism is people depending on their own abilities and skills to get something done. In humanism, the chief resource is what humans can come up with—money, education, organization, morale boosters. Christian humanism is simply doing things for God in our own ability. We speak his name, but we do it with our own resources. The absence of prayer indicates we are attempting to win our city with our own machinations.

When a church has been conditioned to function like this over the years, it is hard to introduce prayer as the primary means of doing the work of God. Without prayer we are basically locked into a "do-it-yourself" Christianity. The opposite of "Christian humanism" is prayer dependence. In prayer, we come before our Father to receive all that is essential to win our city for Christ.

2. Prayer for the city is difficult to establish because prayer is often human-centered, not God-centered. This human-centeredness is evident in two ways. First, we use prayer as a means to get what we want to further our kingdom. James says, "When you ask, you do not receive, because you ask with wrong motives, that you may spend what you get on your pleasures" (James 4:3). When we pray this way, prayer is solely for the benefit of people. Second, hu-

Notes

man-centered prayer tells people "If you pray, you will get something. Do this, pray this way, and you will be enhanced or blessed." Now, I recognize that when we spend time with the Father, we may be blessed or edified. But this is not the reason to pray. We pray to simply please and obey our heavenly Father.

> Fortunately, a few seminaries are now beginning to see the importance of community prayer.

People may ask, "What am I going to get out of being in the prayer room?" The answer is "nothing." This one is for Jesus! We do this out of our love for Jesus Christ. Any other motivation will leave the intercessors disappointed or disillusioned. God-centered prayer simply seeks for God to be glorified in our churches and cities. In John 17 Jesus' prayer is a good example of God-centered praying.

3. Consistent, continual corporate prayer is difficult to establish because so much of our praying today is dependent on feelings. One pastor told me, "I only pray when I feel like it." Corporate prayer is not dependent on emotions or feelings or any other kind of positive experience. Prayer room praying depends on a corporate mentality of discipline and commitment. There will be days when people don't feel like praying. Right up front, we tell people, "Come and pray, whether you feel like it or not."

Prayer is a choice, not a feeling! Paul and Silas probably did not "feel" like praying when they were in the jail at Philippi. They were battered and bruised. Yet, we note that at midnight they "were praying and singing hymns to God" (Acts 16:25). Jesus did not "feel" like praying in the Garden of Gethsemane. Yet, he travailed greatly in prayer. Prayer rooms are not based on feelings that may or may not come. They are based on obedience out of love for Christ. We come to pray because he said, "My house will be called a house of prayer."

4. Community prayer is work because it has been neglected for so many years. Few seminaries and Bible colleges train young men and women to mobilize their churches to pray. One large denomination has a membership of nine million, with 12 major seminaries. Not one of these seminaries has a course on developing the prayer life of the congregation for evangelism and world missions. The largest seminary in the world has only two courses on prayer, and these are electives. With such a void in the training of ministers in prayer, it is little wonder that they fail to see its importance in the church. They are ignorant of practical ways of mobilizing a church to pray for the city.

Fortunately, a few seminaries are now beginning to see the importance of community prayer. For example, Fuller Theological Seminary offers training on how to pray for your city and how to have a prayer ministry in the local church. Dr. Peter Wagner, a professor at Fuller, is on the cutting edge of what is happening in the new prayer movement in the church worldwide. He has written and spoken extensively about this. There is a resistance to prayer rooms simply because people do not realize their importance in Christian tradition and their current rise in the contemporary church movement.

5. Prayer centers are slow to start because people are afraid of group prayer. Corporate prayer has a bad reputation for several reasons. People are afraid a "kook" may come and do something strange to embarrass the church. People are afraid to participate because someone may call on them to pray out loud. A person may have had a bad experience when someone tried to "lay hands" on them or "prophesy"

Notes

over them. Group prayer has also been known to get off on tangents. And, church leaders may fear, "what if we spend time and money, and no one comes!" So for fear of failure or discomfort, we defer the matter to some other church. These objections and fears, founded and unfounded, must be dealt with if a vital center is to happen.

6. Prayer for the city in a prayer place is difficult to start because we live in an instant, fast-food society. As churches we want formulas for quick results. We look for ten steps to church growth. Who wants to risk praying for months without seeing results? Often we are motivated by an attitude of activism where we do things simply because they seem like good ideas or someone else did it and got good results. Instead of just praying, we want to do something, even if it's wrong.

> A vision to reach the city for Christ certainly stretches us beyond ourselves, and that causes us to seek God.

Sometimes, we've acted like Saul in 1 Samuel 13:5-14, when he was facing a battle with the Philistines at Gilgal. The priest, Samuel, was late, like most preachers, in bringing the blessing for battle. Saul was impatient and took matters into his own hands, presenting the offering in Samuel's place. Thus, Saul's reign was cut short because he acted presumptuously. We must not let the desire for quick results cause us to abort a season of prayer essential for spiritual awakening in our cities.

7. Prayer is hard to find when there is a lack of vision for church growth. If we are content with membership, then why pray for the city? Or, sometimes our visions are short sighted. Our goal is simply to meet the budget or pay the denominational dues. For one church in Ohio their major decision for the year was to choose the most biodegradable cup for their fellowship dinners! With little vision, there can be little prayer.

A vision to reach the city for Christ certainly stretches us beyond ourselves and that causes us to seek God. In the book of Acts the disciples went to whole cities to proclaim the Gospel. They had a vision for cities to come to Christ, cities like Lydda, Sharen, Antioch,

Salamis, Paphos, Iconium, Derbe, Lystra, Perga and Attalia. The results of their boldness and preaching were phenomenal. We read in the book of Acts, "On the next Sabbath almost the whole city gathered to hear the word of the Lord" (Acts 13:44). And then later we read, "The word of the Lord spread through the whole region.... And the disciples were filled with joy and with the Holy Spirit" (Acts 13:49, 52). Their goal was not just to found a local church. They wanted to take whole communities for Christ. Such a vision is worthy of the finest expression we can offer up to God.

8. There is resistance to a prayer center because the enemy hates sustained prayer. A sustained, informed, unified prayer force does much damage to his work. The enemy's first priority is to keep people from knowing Jesus as Lord and Savior. He does not want people to enter the Kingdom of God. Therefore, he throws every obstacle imaginable—negativity, unbelief, fear, discouragement, strife—in the way of a prayer center. Prayer undermines his work, breaks his hold on people and brings the Holy Spirit on the scene. You can expect spiritual resistance, but know this: "the one who is in you is greater than the one who is in the world" (1 John 4:4).

Satan has lost. He has only a toothless roar. In Jesus' name we have the advantage. The Lord loves prayer, and he will send resources, remove road blocks and raise up intercessors to pray. Anything the

Notes

enemy hates must be a good thing and worthy of our Lord to accomplish.

> The Lord loves prayer, and he will send resources, remove road blocks and raise up intercessors to pray.

9. Prayer rooms are hard to establish because the church is too busy. The calendar is too full. People are already involved in so much. They may not be excited about giving an hour a week or more. One pastor said, My people are so busy doing church work, they don't have time to pray!"

Granted, the average church is busy, and it may take some time to convince people of the great importance of prayer. Nevertheless, a busy calendar should not prevent a vital prayer ministry. Initially accept those who will pray, expect more and God will add to your number daily those who will pray!

10. Collective, consistent prayer is difficult when there is a lack of Christ-centeredness. The main reason we pray is the wonder and revelation of Jesus. He is the reason we spend time in prayer for our cities. His Word sustains us. His majesty inspires us. His unfolding wonder holds our attention. You may need to pray for a return of his exaltedness to your church in order to pray rightly. The revelation of Jesus will cause people to want to simply come and sit in his presence to worship him and thank him for all he is and does. Without such a vision of Jesus Christ, prayer becomes a religious routine, void of intimacy and fulfillment.

Prayer is Worth It!

Prayer is hard work and it may be disappointing at first. There may be resistance, but the long-term results of such praying are worth it. To see souls saved, churches grow and unity prevail is praiseworthy. To see the crime rate fall, alcoholism decline and teen pregnancies diminish warrants the time and effort to pray. To see a revival of holiness in the high school and a decline in divorces makes the work worthwhile. Pastor after pastor in cities all over the country can testify to the results of ongoing focused prayer in places set apart and designed for such intercession. Make room to pray and see what happens in your community.

Brainstorm

What are the groups in
your church from which
you might recruit people
to pray?

Start thinking of possible prayer captains.

Chapter Seven

Planning a Telephone Prayer Ministry

For years the First Baptist Church of Euless, Texas, has had a telephone in their prayer room to receive calls from hurting people or members. Highland Park United Methodist Church in Dallas, Texas also has a prayer telephone ministry in their Prayer Tower. They receive 150 calls a week from people needing prayer. Many other prayer centers have a number like 696-PRAY or 272-HOPE for people to call to receive prayer. The church in Euless has a toll-free number for the entire metropolitan area. There are several ways to incorporate a telephone ministry into your prayer center. But you should realize that such an addition is a major decision requiring more workers, training and intention.

> There are several ways to incorporate a telephone ministry into your prayer center.

Various Approaches to Telephone Ministry

One option is to have a telephone in the prayer room to communicate requests to those who want to pray. The pastor or prayer coordinator simply puts the requests on a recorder or voice mail that plays them back to anyone who calls. The members of the church can be informed about what to pray for on a daily basis, thus promoting congregational agreement in prayer. It is also very helpful to shut-ins who have time to pray but need to be informed about upcoming events, speakers, budget needs. Members simply call for a list of things to lift up to the Father. It is also possible for them to leave a prayer request on the answering machine or voice mail when they call. This is especially useful in an emergency. Also, members can call when they are out of town and leave an important request if necessary.

This type of telephone ministry works two ways. You can call to learn about concerns or you can have a request or praise report recorded in the prayer room. Such a telephone ministry can be the initial stage of an even bolder prayer outreach using the telephone.

The cell phone has opened up a whole new era for telephone ministry. The cell phone is given to a volunteer who carries it for a designated period of time. Volunteers are trained to answer and pray with those who need prayer. This allows the telephone to be answered 24 hours a day without being on location at a prayer center. This is helpful to smaller churches that may not have the personnel to cover a prayer center 24 hours. To gather prayer requests for the cell phone prayer ministry, one church in Valdosta, Georgia printed on magnets a message that asked for prayer requests and gave the phone number. They place the magnets by pay phones in bowling alleys, taverns and hospital waiting rooms. Imagine what it would be like to be standing by the pay phone at the hospital ready to call the family to report bad news,when you see a number to call for prayer to help you find strength and hope.

> Some churches...use call forwarding after hours when no one is in the prayer room.

Another option is to have someone in the prayer room at all times to answer the telephone to receive prayer requests personally. First United Methodist church of Huntsville, Texas, does this 8 a.m. to 5 p.m. Monday through Friday. Such a telephone ministry is comforting to church members, because they know they can call their church for prayer.

Some churches, like Highland Park United Methodist Church and

Casa View Baptist Church, use call forwarding after hours when no one is in the prayer room. The last person to leave the prayer room simply dials in the telephone number that will receive the next incoming call. Ellen Haines, prayer coordinator at Casa View Baptist, related that one morning about 1 a.m. she received a call from a distressed woman who was suicidal. After prayer and scripture reading, the woman was helped. The woman was a member of the church and is now in Ellen's Sunday school class. Call forwarding works well as long as it is well organized and maintained. All members of the household need to be aware when their telephone is "on call" and be prepared to answer it appropriately.

Finally, some churches advertise a prayer center telephone line in the community for an evangelistic outreach. The Kingsland Baptist Church in Katy, Texas, uses billboards along the interstate highway to advertise their prayer line. This is an excellent way to reach out into the community to touch hurting people.

Problems to Avoid in Telephone Ministry

The problem with a telephone outreach from your prayer center is that the prayer room can be invaded with so many calls that more

time is spent answering the telephone than praying. When this happens, the original intent of the prayer room, to be a place of quiet waiting upon God, is undermined. To solve this problem, it is best to separate the telephone ministry from the prayer room. In other words, have two distinct prayer ministries—one to pray and the other to receive incoming calls and requests. The telephone prayer ministry can be located at the church, or it can utilize call forwarding. People would be recruited to one job or the other.

> This ministry is not meant to give out advice about family conflicts, financial decisions or any other problem.

A telephone prayer ministry is just praying over a telephone with people who have a need or request. This is not a counseling ministry. For legal reasons and time limitations, any kind of telephone counseling should be discouraged. This ministry is not meant to give out advice about family conflicts, financial decisions or any other problem. It is a telephone helpline focusing on prayer.

Remember also that names and needs should be kept confidential. The persons receiving the calls should not give out their names or even tell the caller where they are. The enemy would love to sabotage such a spiritually rich ministry.

For the sake of security, precautions should be taken to protect those who are receiving the calls. The person receiving the calls should have access to emergency numbers such as the pastor, prayer coordinator or captain, law enforcement agencies, fire department, 911, information and other numbers that might be helpful, such as crisis lines for those who may be suicidal. Those receiving the calls must understand their own limitations and be willing to contact the proper helping agency when needed. Again, the purpose of the telephone line is to pray briefly and then record the request for further prayer and evangelistic follow-up if possible. If possible, and if the church is equipped to do so, you may send a team out to the person calling if you have their permission.

Who Should Answer the Phones?

Because this ministry is so vital, only mature, solid Christians should be recruited. The pastor and prayer coordinator can screen the applicants to assure stability and quality in ministry. They need to be good listeners, have a good recall of scripture, not be timid in prayer, sense a vision and burden for this ministry, avoid gossip or sensationalism, have happy family lives and not be given to excesses like preoccupation with the devil. Also, they should be compassionate and non-condemning. They need faith to believe that God is ready and able to help the people who call. Hopefully they are spiritually healthy enough not to need this ministry for their own personal identity. And they need to be team players who work well with the others who are answering the telephone. Beware of "lone rangers" who want things done their way and are critical of others.

> Beware of "lone rangers" who want things done their way and are critical of others.

Notes

Training People to Pray Over the Telephone

Training people to answer the telephone is crucial to a prayer-help telephone ministry. Many people in the local church would love to participate in such a ministry, but they need skills and training. It is best if the training program consists of several sessions that teach and model telephone prayer. Your training session should emphasize the following points.

1. The people who answer the telephone need to prepare themselves before they minister. They need to ask the Holy Spirit to help them be sensitive to the voice of God concerning what to pray. The Holy Spirit serves as a reminder and helper in all kinds of needs. The person praying needs to depend on him for guidance in each call.

2. The person receiving calls needs to be a good listener. How can we pray unless we hear the need? This is important. Answer the call, "Hello, this is the prayer help ministry. What can I pray for you?" Listen carefully and if possible take notes. Later when you pray, callers will know whether you really heard them or are offering a mechanical "canned" prayer. The goal is to convey the compassion of Jesus to the person calling. Jesus was a good listener, and we need to follow his example.

Ask a minimal number of questions to clarify the need for prayer. There are many types of calls concerning a wide range of human needs. Usually, however, a prayer request fits into a certain category:

- Family/Marital Problems

- Financial Needs/Need for Employment

- Mental and Physical Health Needs

- Needs for Forgiveness

- Personal Salvation/The Need for God

- Miscellaneous Needs/Fear, Depression, Guidance

■   Opportunities for Ministry

■   Unexpected Disasters

Remember, intercessors should not gossip or overreact in their response to callers, such as "Oh my," "That's terrible," or "How horrible." If callers share something tragic or shocking such as, "I've just had an abortion," they don't need judgment or the response, "You should not have done that." Pray for the need.

Also, do not try to convert people over the telephone. That may come later, but for now they are calling out of specific needs, and they want prayer. Give the Holy Spirit time to work in their lives. Callers need to know that they are loved, and that in Jesus there is hope. A compassionate, non-condemning listener is apt to lower their guard and help them be open to what the Holy Spirit wants to do in their life. Listen, then pray.

3. When you pray, pray the scriptures over callers' needs. There is great power in God's Word. His Word provides promise in so many ways. Quite often callers are overwhelmed by their distress. It is all that they have been thinking about. Therefore, it is important to pray the answer, not the problem. The training sessions provide an opportunity to learn specific Bible verses and stories that apply to a

Notes

range of needs. These verses need to be given to the intercessors, so that they have an adequate number of verses to choose from in praying for people. The *Prayer Room Intercessors Handbook* (See Resource List) provides some suggested scriptures for various situations. The Word of God should saturate every prayer prayed over the telephone. As mentioned before, Judson Cornwall's book, *Praying The Scriptures*,[17] is a good textbook for the training sessions. This book should be read by the trainers before the training session.

Remember it is important to model the ministry for the trainees. The pastor or coordinator should pray scripture-based prayers in front of trainees to give them an understanding of what this sounds like. It is also helpful to bring a telephone in and act as though you are actually praying for a specific need. Let trainees watch and listen as you pray to give them a feel of scripture-based praying.

A Suggested Telephone-Prayer Outline

It would be good to offer those who will be praying a standard outline to help them pray with confidence and to give structure to the prayer itself. Here is an example:

- Grace

- The Concern

- God's Nature

- His Provision in Jesus

- Receiving the Answer

Grace. We come to the throne of God on the basis of the grace of the Lord Jesus Christ. It is no wonder John wrote, "From the fullness of his grace we have all received one blessing after another. ...grace and truth came through Jesus Christ" (John 1:16-17). And Paul's letters began, "The grace of the Lord Jesus be with you...." We come to God based on the grace of the Lord Jesus Christ.

When we pray it does not matter how good we are, how well we pray, how long we pray, what our track record is or anything else. God's grace alone gives us access to the throne room of God. We come based on who Jesus is and what Jesus did on the cross and in his resurrection. This is important. The need may be great, the person calling may feel bad or guilty or unworthy, but none of this matters—we come based on Jesus Christ. That is why we pray "in Jesus' name." We come to God through Jesus Christ for everything, and

> The answer to the caller's need, dilemma or problem is in Jesus Christ.

this never changes. This emphasis on grace is wonderful because it takes the burden off us—we don't have to worry about getting it just right or feeling like we have failed or let the caller down if we do not feel a certain way. Prayers are heard because of God's grace, not our technique.

The Concerns. In the compassion of Jesus we want callers to know that we have heard their problem or need. After acknowledging God's grace, we simply repeat their petition, as briefly as possible, to let them understand that we understand.

God's Nature. Often people who call have a misconception of who God is and what he is like in regard to their need. If they are hurting,

they could feel he is punishing them. They may think the devil is equally as strong as God. They may think sickness and suffering are his will. They may believe the car wreck was his working. When we pray, it is good to focus on a correct biblical picture of what God is. Examples of how his nature affects our praying are given in the training session.

His provision in Jesus. God's nature is made known to us in Jesus. Everything God is and has done is in his son the Lord Jesus Christ. So when we pray we focus on Jesus. The answer to the caller's need, dilemma or problem is in Jesus Christ. Christ-centered prayer is the ultimate goal of the prayer-help line. When we pray in Jesus, callers can know his comfort, his peace, his presence, his power over fear, his wisdom, his forgiveness. Jesus is the answer for every prayer need.

Receiving the Answer. The last thing to pray is that the person calling will actually receive the hope and life that we are offering in Christ Jesus. This is where it is good to perhaps lead the person in a personal prayer to pray aloud a statement of faith and hope based on what we have said in the above outline. You may say, "Now that I have prayed, would you like for me to lead you in a prayer based on an expectation of God answering us? Just pray after me repeating what I say. Here is an example:

> *Lord Jesus, I now receive from you forgiveness for my family and myself. I thank you for helping me through this crisis, and I trust you to touch my home (or other area prayed for such as work, relationship, body, etc.) in a healing manner. Amen.*

If callers need to repent, lead them in a prayer of repentance. If they need to forgive a specific person, lead them in that prayer. If they need to release a person into God's hands, then lead them in that prayer. It is helpful to lead them in prayer because they have been verbalizing the problem up until now. You can help them verbalize the hope that we have in Christ. Also, by leading them in prayer, you allow them to participate in the answer instead of just listening. If they do not want to pray, simply close the prayer time by asking Jesus to be with them where they are.

This outline is only a suggestion for praying with people. There are certainly many other formats for prayer. The Lord's Prayer is a good outline. Or, you may write your own.

Don't Forget the Details!

Finally, other aspects of prayer help can be covered in the training session such as, DO NOT:

- Pray too loud and long or let callers talk too long.

- Pray so as to confuse or frighten callers.

- Coerce or try to impose your personal feelings.

- Preach or try to get them to come to your church.

- Overreact or feel responsible for callers.

- Ask for money to further the ministry!

Notes

A Sample Training Session

The following training program is an example from one church that recently began a telephone ministry. The session was conducted from 9 a.m. to 12 noon on a Saturday.

9:00 a.m. Begin by stating the vision of the telephone help ministry.

Discuss the power of prayer as a way of reaching the world.

9:30 a.m. Go over the telephone-prayer outline and discuss the biblical basis and intent of such an outline:

- Grace

- The Concern

- The Nature of God

- The Provision of Jesus Christ

- The Prayer of Reception

Offer scriptures related to family problems, parenting, loss of loved ones and other general needs. Do your homework to make these scriptures real to you.

10:15 a.m. Break

10:30 a.m. Model with a real telephone the example of prayer for family problems using scriptures relevant to the needs.

11:30 a.m. Field questions and go over do's and don'ts of the telephone ministry.

11:45 a.m. Pray together to seek God's favor and power upon this ministry.

12:00 a.m. End

Calling the House of Prayer

The potential of such a ministry is far-reaching. In a community of any size, needs will occur in people's lives on a daily basis. They may receive bad news, discover their children are in trouble, incur a sudden illness, experience financial problems, have their homes break up or have their jobs threatened. Or, on a more positive note, job opportunities may become available, babies are born, homes may be purchased or opportunities to witness may come about. Non-Christians and Christians can call to receive prayer. Jesus said, "My house will be called a house of prayer" (Matthew 21:13). What a wonderful fulfillment of this verse when people can call the "house of prayer" for help and comfort.

Brainstorm

A group of smaller churches in Lebanon, Pennsylvania pooled their resources and opened a community prayer room where they plan to have an operating prayer line. By cooperating as the body of Christ they are accomplishing what one small church could not.

Through creative thinking and planning, what model of a prayer line might work in your area?

Chapter Eight

A Plan for City-Wide Prayer

Jesus had a place where he prayed often with his disciples. It was called Gethsemane. This place was across the Kidron Valley from the city of Jerusalem. When I was in Jerusalem I stood in this garden where the Basilica of Agony is now located. This spot offers a panoramic view of the entire city. I believe it was here in this place that Jesus wept and prayed over his city (Luke 19:41). On one occasion he said,

> When Judas betrayed Jesus, he knew where to find him.

> *"O Jerusalem, Jerusalem, you who kill the prophets and stone those sent to you, how often I have longed to gather your children together, as a hen gathers her chicks under her wings, but you were not willing"* (Matthew 23:37).

Perhaps he wept over the temple where money changers and the market place atmosphere denied the presence of God. He was broken over the spiritual blindness of the Pharisees and Sadducees. He could have cried over the plight of the poor and homeless. He possibly prayed, burdened by the sins of addiction, crime and homosexuality.

At any rate, Jesus came often to this place of prayer. When Judas betrayed Jesus, he knew where to find him. We read, "Now Judas, who betrayed him, knew the place, because Jesus had often met there with his disciples" (John 18:2). And of course it was in this place of prayer that Jesus took James, John and Peter and drew apart and greatly agonized over the sins of the world (Mark 14:32-38). It is interesting to note that Jesus was praying here when they came to arrest him and take him to the cross. He began his earthly ministry praying (Mark 1:35) and he concluded it in prayer.

> I believe Jesus has not lost his burden for our cities.

In Austin, Texas, a group of pastors meets once a month in a downtown hotel overlooking the city to pray for their city to come to Christ. In Kenton, Ohio, two pastors pray from the courthouse roof claiming their city for Christ. In Muncie, Indiana pastors meet every other week to ask God to move in their city. I believe Jesus has not lost his burden for our cities because he lives to intercede for our townships and villages (Hebrews 7:25). And I believe he puts this same burden in us. He is looking for someone to stand in the gap. Ezekiel writes, "I looked for a man among them who would build up the wall and stand before me in the gap on behalf of the land so I would not have to destroy it, but I found none" (Ezekiel 22:30). Do you have a burden for your city? Do you have a place to stand in the gap? Will others join you as you pray for your city?

If your desire is to stand in the gap for your city in a place set apart for this purpose, I believe it is helpful to have a prayer strategy or plan to claim your city. Having a God-given plan helps you stay on track as you intercede for your area. It is one thing to say, " Let's take our city for God" and it is another to have a contemplated, advised, one-, two-, or five-year plan to give you direction.

Emotional pleas for prayer are often short-lived. When the conference is over and the crowd dispersed, what will carry you through weeks or months of faithful praise and supplication for the city? Your prayer room may be beautiful and well organized, but what will assure it is in use two years from now?

I believe praying for a city and working for unity, is a long haul proposition. Therefore, a set of rails are needed to carry the vision when feelings and circumstances are contrary to the vision. It is far better to wait for a game plan than to just start and possibly fail. Prayer failures are often hard to resurrect. I would like to share with you a plan to stimulate your creative thinking in developing a plan for your city. Of course this plan may not work for you, but I think it contains some principles that any plan may incorporate.

Divide and Conquer

> Zone praying brings it home to your street, apartment complex, high rise or rural road.

This prayer plan for "taking the city" is called "Divide and Conquer." It will take five years of work to implement this strategy because the city-wide revival is so large it will take a long-range plan to achieve the Father's desire. Unfortunately, we must allow for failure and troop loss.

It is not easy to work for unity and revival in a city. Strongholds have been in place for years and their removal will not be instantaneous. Warfare prayer is taxing to the army. We need to rest after

Notes

battles to regain our strength. Jesus said that we must come in and go out. We were not meant to fight the enemy continually. We need to be renewed; therefore, a long-range plan is essential to keep us intact.

This plan to take the city is named after Joshua's strategy to take the Promised Land. When he crossed the Jordan he divided the land and took city by city, driving out the inhabitants. He eventually established the worship of God at Shiloh (Joshua 18). You can do the same in your city.

First, divide your city into the twelve tribes of Israel and mark a map of the city to reflect this. To say, "We will claim our city for God," sounds good, but in reality it is not realistic or manageable. By dividing your city you can promote "zone praying." In other words, claim where you live, pray for your workplace, school or where you play—the little league park, bowling alley or basketball court. Prayer is hard work, and to bite off too much too soon assures failure. One church in Waco, Texas, tore out pages of the telephone book and gave them out for city-wide prayer. That is much easier to handle than praying over every name in the telephone book. Zone praying brings it home to your street, apartment complex, high rise or rural road.

> We need to pray "smart prayers" that are right on target.

Second, make your plan biblical and fun. Teach your people which tribe they lived in. Put a huge map in the prayer room. For example, Issachar and Zebulun and Napthal are to the north. Downtown is Manasseh. The middle of the city can be divided into Dan, Gad, Ephraim, Asher and Judah. If you have a university or college call it Benjamin, because he was the youngest. Reuben and Simeon are to the south. Teach the meanings of the tribes and how they worked together to take the land. Make banners for them, and give out name tags in the color of each tribe to promote camaraderie and tribal unity.

Biblically, use the theme "Taking the Land" which appears often in the Bible. In fact, the land motif is used 600 times in the Old Testament. In this manner you can take your land personally and corporately! Let us bring our lives under the Lordship of Jesus Christ. This can be your five-year theme for taking your city.

Third, select prayer captains for each tribe. These 12 captains and the leader meet every week to pray for each tribe. These individuals live in or near the tribe and share this vision and burden for the city. Their main job is to pray over their area of the city. Later, lieutenants can be added to the street prayer warriors. These persons are accountable to the captains and take specific prayer assignments, such as the shopping mall, the high schools, the hospitals, large apartment complexes or dormitories.

Fourth, the captains provide a profile of each tribe for the prayer room. The profile tells you what is in each tribal area so you can pray accordingly. For example, maybe the tribe of Dan is rough with crack cocaine houses, drug deals and bars. There are strongholds that control some of the people in affluence, and some of the residents are caught up in worldly concerns. There might also be a hospital and a Church of the Latter Day Saints there. Judah has the regional shopping mall and attracts people from a 50-mile radius. Judah also has a high school where there are strongholds of immorality and drug usage. The profile of each tribe helps you pray for your city in an informed and specific manner.

Notes

In the Persian gulf war they used "smart bombs." We all watched in amazement as bombs went down elevator shafts, smoke stacks and through air vents. Whereas in previous wars bombs were dropped from 20,000 feet to hit whatever, smart bombs went right to the designated target. We need to pray "smart prayers" that are right on target. By knowing your city you can divide and conquer and be more responsible to pray. Plus, it is helpful to know the enemy and his strongholds and how they got there. As we divided our city we could discern strongholds of rationalism, rebellion, divorce, immorality, Satanism and idolatry. Joshua knew who his enemy was, and we must know our enemy if we are to undo his gates and free the captives.

Also list the churches in your city so they can be soaked in prayer in the prayer room. In addition, target "people groups" such as physicians, attorneys, street gangs, construction crews, senior citizens and law enforcement officials. Pray for major breakthroughs into these special groups of people.

> Remember, the purpose of warfare prayer is more effective evangelism.

Put pictures in your prayer room of the high schools, city hall, courthouse, jail and police departments. It helps to visualize as you pray.

Encourage your people to walk and pray. In Joshua 1:3 we read, "I will give you every place where you set your foot, as I promised Moses." So walk each tribal area and claim it for Christ. Have high school students walk around their high schools on Tuesday and Thursday mornings. They can take their land for Christ. Those who walk in the shopping mall for exercise can begin to claim the area for Christ. Some may drive around the city on "Jericho drives." Others may walk their streets praying for the unchurched.

Sixth, teach and practice the principles of spiritual warfare in order to take your land. Paul wrote, "For our struggle is not against flesh and blood, but against the rulers, against the authorities, against the powers of this dark world and against the spiritual forces of evil in the heavenly realms" (Ephesians 6:12). Understand who your enemies are and how they entered your city as controlling spirits. State the goal of your warfare: the release of the captives! Remember, the purpose of warfare prayer is more effective evangelism (Matthew 16:18). Bind the darkness in order to loosen the captives that they may be saved. Our desire is not to give the devil undue attention. We want the lost to be found. As a part of our warfare, we are calling the church to holiness and repentance.

An unholy church cannot drive out an unholy enemy. A divided church cannot drive out a unified enemy. We want God's presence in us as a body to undo the strongholds in our cities. Therefore, warfare was not and is not a lone church issue. It is something we must do together if we are to take our city for God. Plan to incorporate as many churches as possible in your frontal attack upon the enemy.

As a part of warfare strategy teach the weapons of our warfare: the Name of Jesus, the Word of God, the blood of the Lamb, the righteousness of Jesus Christ. Teach the importance of praise and worship to pull down strongholds. Hold tribal praise meetings in parks to take the battle to his turf to gain regional victory. When I led the church I pastored through this plan we distributed praise tapes before these rallies to help soften the territory. Always pray a hedge of protection around the pastors and churches of your city.

You must recognize that we are in this for the long run and we

Notes

simply go step by step, precept by precept. We fight, and we rest. After every major battle Joshua went back to Gilgal and rested the troops. It is also important to retain what we gain. We must disciple those who are won so that they are truly made disciples.

A Report From the Front Line

Mario Murillo, author of *Critical Mass*[23], is right—if you pray for revival you had better plan for a way to handle and disciple the harvest.

When our church implemented this plan, after two years of praying, we saw our crime rate drop 17 percent! The mayor of one of our cities professed faith in Christ and was baptized! The shopping mall manager professed faith in Christ and was baptized into Christ. Pastors began praying together for our city.

> The Holy Spirit will honor your efforts to make room for prayer.

We hosted concerts of prayer where churches of different denominations came together for corporate prayer. Several hundred people attended these meetings including, Southern Baptists, United Methodists, Catholics, Assembly of God and independent churches. We saw professions of faith every Sunday in our church! MTV was removed from our local cable television and provided on a request only basis.

Strongholds of denominational antagonism were broken and removed. People confessed their sins. Pastors affirmed one another and recognized their need for each other. Congregations laid down their cultural preferences and distinctions to learn to love and appreciate each other. There are now four prayer centers in that city.

I believe the principle of Divide and Conquer works. There will be failures and disappointments, but move forward to take the land. Although you will need to tailor the plan for your areas, I offer it to you as a suggestion to stir up your own sanctified imagination to envision a plan to take your city.

We have constructed a 14-session workbook that teaches how to gain a new focus for prayer. *Blueprint for the House of Prayer* is a valuable tool for bringing new life and understanding to the prayer ministry of your church (See Resource List). When there is lack of understanding...teach. You cannot wage war on your knees until those who are praying have a clear understanding of the objective.

The Holy Spirit will honor your efforts to make room for prayer. Laborers will come. Barriers will fall. Bridges will be built. Why? Because the place and principle of Gethsemane will always be in the heart of Jesus. He came then and he comes now to seek and save our lost cities. "For the Son of Man came to seek and to save what was lost" (Luke 19:10).

"Therefore, my dear brothers, stand firm. Let nothing move you. Always give yourselves fully to the work of the Lord, because you know that your labor in the Lord is not in vain"(1 Corinthians 15:58).

Notes

Brainstorm

List twelve distinctive areas
of your city. Colleges,
industrial parks, etc. can
be considered areas.

Chapter Nine

What Are We Going to Do With the Junk?

I will never forget the moment. Our church had decided to make room to pray. We were going to put the prayer center in a room just off the sanctuary that was being used for storage.

One day I was showing a man in the church the room and explaining what we were planning to do. I opened the door and turned on the light. The room was full of junk: broken chairs, recreation equipment, scraps of carpet from the building program, Christmas decorations, past drama props, odds and ends and an old safe whose combination we had lost.

"We are going to put a twenty-four hour prayer ministry in this room," I said. "Imagine—people coming here to pray around the clock! I'm so excited."

He responded, "Yes, Pastor, prayer is fine, but what are you going to do with all this junk?"

> If you are going to make room to pray, you have to get rid of some junk!

He had a good question. If you are going to make room to pray you have to get rid of some junk! What I mean is that you need to make room in your heart first, and then you need to make room in your church's heart if together you are going to pray in a magnanimous manner. Mother Teresa said, "Prayer enlarges the heart for God." If this is true, then we need to do some house cleaning or heart cleaning if we are to pray effectively. The junk has got to go. How can we claim our cities if our own hearts and churches are unclaimed before God?

Broken Faith

What is the junk in your church's closet? And how do you get rid of it? Some churches have broken faith instead of broken chairs. Joshua 7:2 says that Israel broke faith with God. Our hearts must be cleansed of doubt if we are going to pray for our city, because faith makes prayer work. Jesus said, "If you believe, you will receive whatever you ask for in prayer" (Matthew 21:22). Even Jesus had limited success in his own hometown because of unbelief. The Bible says, "And he was amazed at their lack of faith" (Mark 6:6). We can have a great prayer room, nice carpet, pretty drapes and adequate information, but if we harbor unbelief in our hearts we will not take our own lives, much less the city, for God. Mistrust of God and even each other has got to go in the dumpster.

> If we harbor unbelief in our hearts we will not take our own lives, much less the city, for God.

Ask Jesus to help your unbelief. Admit your doubts. Repent of worry, fear and unhealthy natural reasonings. Let the Holy Spirit scan your heart to expose any "broken faith." Faith is a gift (Romans 12:3) that is strengthened by hearing the Word of God (Romans 10:17). Make room in your heart for faith, and as you enter the prayer center your prayers will make a difference.

Serious Business

We also took out the junk play equipment, because this whole matter of prayer is serious business. We cannot play at praying. It requires our very best. Souls are at stake; the city needs a spiritual awakening; there is a clash between kingdoms over your city. Therefore, we must have serious intent in our hearts. It was said of Epaphras, "who is one of you and a servant of Christ Jesus.... He is always wrestling in prayer for you that you may stand firm in all the will of God, mature and fully assured" (Colossians 4:12).

Sometimes prayer is like a wrestling match in which we struggle with our own apathy or lethargy. We sometimes feel pressed by busy schedules and complicated lives. We may even feel the press of powers opposed to God. Therefore a serious call to prayer and a holy life are in order. Allow God to remove from your heart any casual, take-it-or-leave-it attitude. Petition Jesus to give you a seriousness about prayer. Ask him to rekindle your heart to the level of passion you felt when you first believed. As you make room in your heart for fervent intercession, prayer time in the prayer room will be something you desire.

Tossing Out the "Scraps"

While preparing our prayer room we removed scraps of carpet from our storage room. Every church has "church scraps" or fights from past disagreements. Some churches are more "scrappy" than others.

The hurt, resentment or bitter feelings can stop a heart from vital prayer. It is hard to intercede for someone you do not like. Maybe the pastor said or did something, perhaps a deacon voted you off a committee or the board spent too much on candles. Whatever the garbage, it needs to go at the foot of the cross. If we are to pray, we must forgive and forgive and forgive. The goal of corporate prayer is agreement. Jesus said, "If two agree." Agreement produces strength in a prayer ministry. Fault-finding and criticizing only clutter the heart or the church. Put these feelings, hurts and angry memories in the dumpster and shut the lid. Focus on Jesus and his love. Ask him for forgiveness and for the ability to give forgiveness. Remember, he washed Judas' feet during the Last Supper. Make room in your heart, and the prayer room will be filled with his presence.

> If we are to pray, we must forgive and forgive and forgive.

Repenting of Pride

As we cleaned out that storage room, our church also threw out drama props and decorations from past church pageants. To make room to pray we must throw out the pride of past successes and giant program productions. Pride needs to be discarded. Prayer thrives on Christlike humility, a teachable spirit and a genuine seeking of God. In the upper room the disciples were not proud of the resurrection because the Pharisees and Sadducees were proved wrong and they were right. Jesus' followers prayed continually knowing that only in complete dependence upon the Lord would they succeed. Fix your attention on Jesus. Repent of desiring larger numbers, better buildings or more correct doctrine. Ask Jesus to cleanse your heart of denominational pride. A good prayer for us might be:

> *Lord, forgive our hearts when we just want to be good Methodists, Baptists or Pentecostals. Help us to be kingdom seekers and not status seekers. Remove from our hearts the refuse of self-sufficiency, complacency and isolationism. In your name, set us free. Amen.*

Petty Junk

Our storage room also had a lot of petty junk, small stuff that did not amount to anything. Does your church have a petty junk collection? Look in your heart. Do you desire recognition or reward? Do you always want to be right? Do you love minorities? Are you patient toward the sinner, yet firm with the sin? Do you fight in meetings and play "one-upmanship?" Do you argue over which room to use? Are you bent out of shape because the choir director asks "her" to sing the special? Are you upset because "their" kid got the award? Are you going to leave church if they do not take out the drums? The petty junk in our hearts must be confessed.

> Haul out petty concerns and make room for China, Albania, the ghetto or the unborn who face abortion.

Lord, have mercy on our petty clutter and cleanse our hearts so we can pray. Give us pure hearts so we can see God. Change our small perspective. Jesus, show us the plight of the poor in our cities, help us to understand the boredom and loneliness of teenagers. Lord, break our hearts

Notes

*with what breaks your heart. Father, burden us
with your burden. Lord, have mercy and please
do not deal with us according to our
prayerlessness.*

Haul out the petty concerns and make room for China, Albania, the ghetto or the unborn who face abortion.

The Riskiness of Prayer

Finally, we threw out the safe whose combination we had lost. It was the last of the junk. How about it? In our hearts do we want to play it "safe"? Do we cling to our own personal and corporate security, keeping it locked in our hearts? Do we want a nice, neat, well-oiled program with no disruptions?

> Prayer puts the status quo in jeopardy.

This desire for safety is junk that has to go. It is unsafe to pray. It is a risk to comfort. It is a risk to our neatness. Peter was on the roof trying to take a nap and pray a little, and he ended up taking the Gospel to the Gentiles (Acts 10). Prayer puts the status quo in jeopardy. When we pray, Jesus speaks, admonishes, leads, stops, guides, corrects, blesses, gives, takes, convicts, convinces, changes, rules and overrules. What we want to make way for is his will and kingdom. Prayer is powerful and could even start a riot! (Acts 16:16-23).

Make room in your heart to pray. Nail your love of security and your fear of failure to the cross. Pray for boldness in place of blindness. Repent of sameness, lameness and tameness. Put out the things that quench the Spirit. As a church, leave the safety of the placidly predictable. Remove attitudes and opinions that keep you passive and passionless. As a church, flee from the danger of wanting to be thought well of by everyone. Make room in your heart to pray. Ask the Holy Spirit to put you on the cutting edge of music, evangelism and prophetic preaching. Let Jesus come and confront the sin of your city with your witness. Then and only then will your prayer room become a serious threat to the principalities and powers over your town.

Making Room in Our Hearts for Prayer

There may be other items that need to go to the dumpster. Ask God and he will show you the junk. He has the power to cleanse and forgive.

Making room to pray individually or corporately is one thing. But making room in our hearts for prayer is the crucial matter, because God sees the attitude of the heart. For if God finds that we have a place in our hearts in which to pray, then having a place to pray in the church takes on a deeper meaning.

Notes

Brainstorm

Do you intend to begin a
prayer room ministry?

What are the first three steps?

1.

2.

3.

Notes

1. Michael Green, *First Things Last*, (Nashville: Discipleship Resources, 1979), page 91.

2. Warren Wiersbe, *Something Happens When Churches Pray*, (Lincoln, Nebraska: Back To the Bible) page 38.

3. Paul Y. Cho, *Prayer: Key to Revival*, (Dallas: Word Publishing), page 44.

4. John Dawson, *Taking Our Cities For God*, (Lake Mary, Florida: Creation House, 1989).

5. Michael Green, *First Things Last*, page 91.

6. Michael Green, *First Things Last*, page 92.

7. Dick Eastman, *The Hour that Changes the World*, (Grand Rapids: Baker Book House, 1978), page 158-161.

8. John Wimber, *Power Evangelism*, (San Francisco: Harper & Row, 1986), page 44.

9. Thomas D. Elliff, *Praying For Others*, (Nashville: Broadman Press, page 13).

10. Francis Frangipane, *The House of the Lord*, (Lake Mary, Florida: Creation House, 1991), page 39.

11. Martyn Lloyd-Jones, *Joy Unspeakable*, (Wheaton: Harold Shaw Publishers, 1984).

12. Michael Green, *First Things Last*, pages 87-88.

13. Dr. Alvin J. Vander Griend, *The Praying Church Sourcebook*, (Grand Rapids: Church Development Resources).

14. Judson Cornwall, *Praying the Scriptures*, (Altamonte Springs, Florida: Creation House).

15. Dick Eastman, *The Hour That Changes the World*.

16. Maxie Dunham, *The Workbook of Living Prayer*, (Nashville: The Upper Room, 1974).

17. Judson Cornwall, *Praying the Scriptures*.

18. Mario Murillo, *Critical Mass*, (Chatsworth, California: Anthony Douglas Publishing Co).

Resource List

Prayer Room Intercessors Handbook
ISBN: 1-57892-049-3
> A guide book for those who pray in the prayer room.

Pray the Price Resource Kit
ISBN: 1-57892-042-6
> A loose leaf reproducible manual that contains 10 prayer guides, 5 door hangers, prayer-line note cards, sign up sheets, prayer request forms, and many other prayer room supplies.

Blueprint for the House of Prayer
ISBN: 1-57892-043-4
> 14 lessons that include prayer assignments. A good place to start a small group on a "new prayer" adventure.

Acts 29, Fifty Days to Invite the Holy Spirit
ISBN: 1-57982045-0
> A corporate or individual prayer journey through the book of Acts. Through prayer, write the 29th chapter of Acts for your city.

Pray the Price, United Methodists United In Prayer
ISBN: 1-57892-041-8
> The heart and soul of the call to prayer. Discussion questions at the end of each chapter enable a small group to come to a new understanding of our need to pray.

Your Pastor: Preyed On or Prayed For
ISBN: 1-57892-044-2
> How to hedge your pastor and the pastoral family in prayer. A prayed for pastor is an effective pastor.

Keys to the Kingdom:
  Prayers For My Pastor ISBN: 1-57892-005-1
  Prayers For My Children ISBN: 1-57892-008-6
  Prayers For My Husband ISBN: 1-57892-007-8
  Prayers For My Wife ISBN: 1-57892-006-X
  Prayers For Healing ISBN: 1-57892-009-4
  Personal Prayers: Praying My Identity In Christ ISBN: 1-57892-047-7
> Each Key ring holds 40 Scripture based prayers. Since they are the size of a business card they fit in a briefcase, a purse or on the dash of the car.

For a complete listing of prayer resources call toll free: (888) 656-6067